DARE TO BE CHRISTIAN

Developing a Social Conscience

Bernard Häring, C.SS.R.

LIGUORI
PUBLICATIONS

One Liguori Drive
Liguori, Missouri 63057
(314) 464-2500

Imprimi Potest:
John F. Dowd, C.SS.R.
Provincial, St. Louis Province
Redemptorist Fathers

Imprimatur:
Monsignor Edward J. O'Donnell
Vicar General, Archdiocese of St. Louis

ISBN 0-89243-180-6
Library of Congress Catalog Card Number: 83-80956

Scripture texts are taken from *The New English Bible*. © The Delegates of the Oxford University Press and the Syndics of the Cambridge University Press 1961, 1970. Reprinted by permission.

Excerpts from *Vatican Council II: The Conciliar and Post Conciliar Documents*, edited by Austin Flannery, O.P., copyright 1975, used by permission of Costello Publishing Co., Northport, N.Y. 11768.

Cover design by Pam Hummelsheim
Cover photo by Photofile

Published simultaneously in England under a different title for the British Commonwealth, not including Canada. This North American edition is to be sold only in Canada and the United States of America.

Table of Contents

Acknowledgments

My heartfelt thanks to Mrs. Josephine Ryan who, with her usual generosity and competence, polished my English and typed this text. My thanks extend also to her friend, Marion McCracken, who checked the textual references and the typescript.

INTRODUCTION

Some time ago the president of the University of Munich, Professor Nikolaus Lobkowicz, was asked what kind of changes the world needs most to encourage belief in God and the attainment of peace. His response was prompt: "Radiant saints! . . . They recognize the 'signs of the times.' Without saints nothing really new and authentic will happen. True saints are people whom God has seized and graced; but usually saints arise only where the awareness prevails that striving for holiness is an integral element of being Christian."

These pages are written to strengthen that consciousness. My book *In Pursuit of Holiness* concludes with a chapter entitled "Becoming Missionaries of Holiness." Many people imagine that saints are persons who simply withdraw from the world to pursue nothing more than their own salvation or quietude. We know, however, that being "chosen," being called to holiness — called, indeed, to follow Christ — is an offer open to all humankind. Holiness, in a distinctively Christian sense, cannot be privatized. Hence, my aim here is to present in tangible form the essential social dimension of being Christian. Jesus told his disciples to "go forth to every part of the world and proclaim the Good News to the whole creation" (Mark 16:15). And Vatican II, in speaking of the goals to be achieved by the laity, says that — led by the light of the Gospel — they are to renew the temporal order in such a way that it can be brought into conformity with the higher principles of Christian life (see *Laity,* 7).

There is also a special need to awaken the sensitivity of all Christians to this dimension, in view of some absurd "theological" assertions which give first importance or almost exclusive attention to the need for *revolutionary* changes of structure. Some would even advocate violence as the prime instrument for saving the world, despite all the evidence that violence begets more violence and hatred and, in today's world, can lead to the utter destruction of the human race.

What the world needs now is people who *dare to be Christian* in everyday life.

1
SEEK THE TRUTH

Jesus replied [to Pilate], "My kingdom does not belong to this world. If it did, my followers would be fighting to save me from arrest by the Jews. My kingly authority comes from elsewhere." "You are a king, then?" said Pilate. Jesus answered, " 'King' is your word. My task is to bear witness to the truth. For this I was born; for this I came into the world, and all who are not deaf to truth listen to my voice." Pilate said, "What is truth?" and with these words went out again to the Jews. "For my part," he said, "I find no case against him" (John 18:36-38).

The world needs people who seek truth, the ultimate meaning of life — salvation truth. It needs people who pursue it in an honest exchange of genuine convictions in discussion with others.

Mature Christians know that Christ is *the Truth*. For them, the one thing that matters is to know Christ and, through him, the Father, thus coming to know ever better the origin, destiny, and vocation of God's people.

Holy people know that salvation truth is not exclusively their own. Seized by Christ and blessed by the unsurpassable knowledge of Christ, they realize that the world needs nothing more urgently than this truth, this knowledge. Their own striving for a more profound, more encompassing and vital knowledge of truth goes hand in hand, therefore, with their desire to pass it on to others and help them on the road to truth.

Today's world is in a situation similar to that of Pilate and the ruling class of Israel: Their interest in truth and their allegiance to it are dangerously off target.

Faced with the greatest decision in human history, Israel's ruling class and the representative of Roman world power are thoroughly immersed in the quest for earthly power. They see truth and justice only in the perspective of their own main interests. They are unwilling and, in a certain sense, already unable to deal directly with truth and justice. A truth that does not serve their interests leaves them skeptical. For them, even their religion is viewed as an instrument of power. Thus their access to saving truth is blocked, as is also the pathway to justice.

Before them stands the powerless witness of the saving truth, the Truth in person. Yet through this powerlessness shines the divine majesty of salvation truth, incarnate in Jesus Christ who will seal it with his blood as Redeemer.

Facing the Divine Truth

The "I-am-the-Truth" of John's Gospel shows us that the vital decision of every person, and of humanity as a whole, is made in confrontation with the truth for which they stand, for which they live and die. "All who are not deaf to truth listen to my voice" (John 18:37).

When we face the "I-am-the-Truth" and his authentic witnesses, there is no legitimate escape into mere theoretical questions. We all must make a decision about our own truth of existence; and, in doing so, we reveal either our adherence to truth or our alienation from it. Jesus tells the Jews in scathing language why his teaching "makes no headway with you" (John 8:37). They have made themselves slaves of the "father of lies" (John 8:45) in whom there is no truth; therefore, they are carrying out their own "father's desires" (John 8:44). But those who sincerely seek the saving truth and act accordingly are at home with the words of Jesus; they rejoice in hearing his voice.

The fundamental option to seek ultimate truth and meaning and to act on them clears the way for the blessed reign of truth; and this liberating experience of ever-new horizons of truth helps us better appreciate "I-am-the-Truth."

With all the ardor of his love and in full awareness of his being sent by the Father, Jesus speaks about this mystery of God and man. "This is eternal life: to know thee who alone art truly God, and Jesus Christ whom thou hast sent" (John 17:3).

Exultingly he announces the happiness of those who have entered into this realm of knowledge and truth. "I have taught them all that I learned from thee, and they have received it: they know with certainty that I came from thee; they have had faith to believe that thou didst send me" (John 17:8). And at the same time he prays fervently for his disciples, that they may loyally proclaim this truth to the world which so badly needs it. "Consecrate them by the truth. . . . may they all be one: as thou, Father, art in me, and I in thee, so also may they be in us, that the world may believe that thou didst send me" (John 17:18,21).

Attainment of this saving truth comes not from mere human effort; it is the work of the Spirit of Truth. By their fundamental option, made with heart, mind, and will, the disciples of Christ open themselves to the promptings of the Holy Spirit. "I will ask the Father, and he will give you another to be your Advocate, who will be with you for ever — the Spirit of truth. The world cannot receive him, because the world neither sees nor knows him; but you know him, because he dwells with you and is in you" (John 14:16-17).

The "world" of which Jesus speaks is that of people locking themselves into their own pride, trusting in their own achievement. This is true of the people of today's world who seem unable to rise above the realm of experimental knowledge, of truth sought only for utility's sake.

Listening to the Spirit of Truth

This world is to be changed, to be offered a new chance by the disciples of Christ. Seized by the Spirit of Truth, they will be gradually led into the full truth. "Your Advocate, the Holy Spirit whom the Father will send in my name, will teach you everything, and will call to mind all that I have told you" (John 14:26). The word "everything" in this quotation does not mean an encyclopedic knowledge but rather an encompassing vision of reality in the light of Christ's Gospel. And that is what the world of today so urgently needs.

Through Christ's faithful disciples who entrust themselves to the power of the Spirit of Truth, this very Spirit "will confute the world, and show where wrong and right and judgment lie" (John 16:8). Even those who rely only on their own strength will finally be able to see their error, their alienation, when faced with Christ's true disciples who are determined to seek God's kingdom and, therefore, are filled with joy, peace, and love. Those who seek only their own interest, power, and "right," will come to realize how far they are from righteousness and truth. Their restless and ruthless search for more power, more possessions, more consumption will be seen in very truth as bringing misery to themselves and others while alienating them from saving and all-encompassing truth and justice (see John 16:8-13).

From people who are guided by the Spirit of God, the "Father of the poor," all men of good will can learn that they cannot dwell in the truth unless they effectively take sides with the unloved, the oppressed, the downtrodden.

Those who are on the pathway of truth will understand ever better that, for their own salvation as well as for the sake of humanity, they still have to go a long way before they are completely transformed in their whole being and all their relationships by the truth. But grace calls to them and comes to them. "His divine power has bestowed on us everything that makes for life and true religion, enabling us to know the One who called us by his own splendour and might. Through this might and splendour he has given us his promises, great beyond all price, and through them you may escape the corruption with which lust has infected the world, and come to share in the very being of God.

"With all this in view, you should try your hardest to supplement your faith with virtue, virtue with knowledge, knowledge with self-control, self-control with fortitude, fortitude with piety, piety with brotherly kindness, and brotherly kindness with love" (2 Peter 1:2-7).

Our concern, then, must be that our knowledge of our Lord Jesus Christ will not be useless or barren for the life of the world (see 2 Peter 1:8), but rather fruitful in truth and love. God is love, and we are to be his image. Salvation knowledge leads us on the pathway of love, and as we progress in saving love we are led to a deeper and more blessed knowledge of truth.

The Wisdom of Truth

The apostle of the Gentiles rejoices that he is privileged to impart not the wisdom of the rulers of his time but "God's hidden wisdom, his secret purpose framed from the very beginning to bring us to our full glory" (1 Corinthians 2:7).

While today's situation is in many ways different from that of Paul's time, it is an astounding and alarming sign of our times that the so-called "developed" world schools its people mainly in the area of acquiring material goods and in the exercise of domination, especially the practice of right by might. The whole educational system of the Western World seems geared to economic, professional, and social success. Because of this, the achievers and consumers which this system graduates are out of sync with the wisdom that comes from God and leads to God.

Granted, structural changes of our system are surely necessary, but they will not succeed without men and women outstanding in wisdom. Christians have to become more aware of what they can and must give to the world if they are to be faithful to their calling. "This is the Spirit that we have received from God, and not the spirit of the world, so that we may know all that God, of his own grace, has given us; and because we are interpreting spiritual truths to those who have the Spirit, we speak of these gifts of God in words found for us not by our human wisdom but by the Spirit'' (1 Corinthians 2:12-13).

The wisdom which concerns us is not speculation about theories entirely foreign to our everyday life but wisdom about the destiny and calling of men and women, understood in the light of the love of the Creator and Redeemer. The Second Vatican Council speaks about this in regard to our vocation to holiness. ''Christ, who died and was raised up for the sake of all, can show man the way and strengthen him through the Spirit in order to be worthy of his destiny: nor is there any other name under heaven given among men by which they can be saved. The Church likewise believes the key, the center and the purpose of the whole of man's history is to be found in its Lord and master'' (*Church in the Modern World,* 10).

We should not think that the saints, whom humankind needs so much today, are concerned exclusively with the supernatural. Their scale of values encompasses a wholeness of vision in which all the different kinds of knowledge have their own weight and place.

As Christians, we are open-minded to every kind of truth. We learn from humanity's historical experience made accessible to us through scientific research. We cannot ignore the natural sciences that unfold many secrets — processes that explain the give-and-take of the created world. They not only help us to admire ever more God's wonderful work but also are indispensable for human health, food production, and many other human needs. Nor can we ignore the behavioral sciences which improve our understanding of human development, psychic growth, and social relationships.

When Christian men and women make their contribution in such fields as culture, science, economics, politics, education, the healing professions, they have to do their very best to acquire the necessary competence. Piety and good will alone are not enough.

The authentic Christian will be distinguished from the unbelieving and uninformed person by his or her priorities and vision of wholeness. Salvation truth comes first: to know God and to know people in the light of Christ. And Christians should never forget that salvation knowledge cannot be acquired in the same ways as knowledge for material success and the exercise of domination. Since God is love, and since our vocation is to be and to become ever more an image of God, the genesis and progression on our pathway of salvation truth depend on the firmness and depth of our fundamental option for redeemed and redeeming love.

This insight was sharply brought home to me by an experience in a leprosarium in India. There I met a young and gifted artist from Paris, France. When she, who had been brought up in total atheism, began to ask and discuss religious questions, a young man told her one day with astonishing conviction: "The God in whom we believe cannot be found by mere reasoning and discussion. Since he is Love, he can be found only by loving people."

She told us that those words affected her deeply, so much so that she kept asking herself: "But how can I be sure that what I intend to do is really done for love's sake?" She decided then, on the spur of the moment, to serve for one year in the rehabilitation of lepers in India, especially because of her terrible distaste for this kind of misery. At the end of the year she chose to remain there in gratitude to God and to these poor people, since they had helped her to find God — to find love.

Our Devotion to Truth

Our devotion to truth implies a wonderful wholeness which we can describe as: *being truthful, thinking truthfully, speaking and acting truthfully.*

Being truthful: The world, deceived by so many ideologies, power structures, collective and individual egotisms, is in dire need of our being truthful — "being in the truth."

We can dialogue as Christians only if we have found and are living our identity, our *yes* to the saving truth in Jesus Christ. To "be in the truth" implies an absolutely sincere conscience — a conscience formed in truthfulness to God and ourselves, matured in open discussion with others who seek the truth, and acted out in everyday affairs. Further, it implies fidelity, reliability, and total commitment to "act out the truth in love." This truthfulness and clarity of conscience coincide with the "purity of heart," the purity of intentions and motives, so highly praised in the Sermon on the Mount.

As pilgrims we cannot "be in the truth" without humbly acknowledging that we are, at best, only on the road to greater fullness of truthfulness in being and in acting. This gives us the courage to confess our sins and shortcomings and to accept the need for further conversion to the One who can say, "I-am-the-Truth," while praising God constantly for having called us into his wonderful light.

Thinking truthfully: People whose thinking has become superficial, confused — even chaotic — can be helped greatly by contact with persons whose minds and hearts are filled with the exhilarating truth revealed in Jesus Christ. These persons give priority to salvation truth, and cultivate other forms of knowledge according to their scale of values and of service to love and justice. Above and beyond the study of what promotes their own material progress and success, they take care to know God, to recognize Christ, to understand human dignity and destiny — all because of their love of truth. And, out of gratitude for the knowledge received from God and through other people, they strive for ever deeper and more integrated knowledge.

A person who wants to think truthfully will also develop a contemplative dimension of human life, arranging for quiet times, and being temperate in the search for news and information, with discernment for the things that are truly worth considering.

Speaking and acting truthfully go hand in hand. People's faces radiate either their purity of heart and mind or, on the contrary, they reveal their frustration, restlessness, hostility of thought and intention. Our actions are highly qualified communications. If they arise from our being in the truth and thinking the truth in love, they generate healthy relationships and build up community in truth.

As Christians, we speak truth only insofar as we speak with authentic love and in the service of love and justice. Our truthful words and actions resemble the Word Incarnate who, from all eternity, is that WORD which breathes love and sends us the Spirit of Truth, enabling us to act out the truth in love.

Whoever uses acquired knowledge to hurt or damage others is not in the truth, does not think truthfully, does not speak the truth. Abuse of information is allied to the work of the "confuser" (the devil). Only truth spoken and acted upon in love comes from God and leads to God, the Father of light.

The service of truth requires discretion, prudence, discernment. True disciples of Christ are discreet about what they say and to whom they say it (see Matthew 7:6). When dealing with people who ask questions whose answers would bring harm to us or others, then this situation partially determines the meaning and manner of our discourse. Against such evil intentions, a word concealing what has to be concealed does not contradict the basic rule imparted to us by Christ: "Plain 'Yes' or 'No' is all you need to say" (Matthew 5:37).

Our refusal to participate in the malice of others is a firm *yes* to our mission to be the "salt to the world," a firm *no* to the reign of darkness and the work of the "confuser." This can be exemplified by the response — given by Christian nurses during the reign of Hitler — to the hangmen who asked at their orphanage about the number of children under their care who were affected by hereditary diseases. What they were really asking was not about sick children in need of help but simply about victims for the gas chambers and soap factories. The Sisters' response to that real question could only be, "We have no such children." Holiness has nothing to do with naïvety.

Prayer

Lord Jesus Christ, before your sacrificial death you prayed for us to the Father: "Sanctify them in the truth!"

Send forth the Holy Spirit to lead us into a growing knowledge of your love and truth, a loving knowledge of the Father and a saving knowledge of ourselves and our brothers and sisters.

Cleanse our hearts, our minds, our wills through the Spirit of Truth. Help us to strive toward an ever fuller knowledge of our faith and all that it implies. Gather us together in your name, so that we can assist each other in our love for truth and our joy in the saving truth.

Help us to rid ourselves of senseless curiosity about thousands of petty things, and teach us to ignore all news which contributes nothing to our growth or our mission and ministry. Assist and illumine us in our striving for whatever knowledge is necessary for skillful service to others.

Remind those who — with all their learning — seem to know nothing about justice, love, and salvation that they are blind and are ignorant of truth. Grant them hunger and thirst for the essential truths.

With you, Lord Jesus, we praise the Father for having revealed the secrets of salvation to the simple ones while they remain hidden from the arrogant who boast about their wisdom (see Luke 10:21). Through the power of the Spirit of Truth, help us to seek the truth honestly and sincerely. Teach us to learn from the humble and the poor.

2
BE OPEN TO DIALOGUE

Never remain silent when a word might put things right,
for wisdom shows itself by speech,
and a man's education must find expression in words.
Do not argue against the truth. . . .
Never be ashamed to admit your mistakes. . . .

Be quick to listen,
but take time over your answer.
Answer a man if you know what to say,
but if not, hold your tongue.
Honour or shame can come through speaking,
and a man's tongue may be his downfall.
Do not get a name for being a gossip
or lay traps with your tongue. . . .

Do not answer without first listening,
and do not interrupt when another is speaking.

One man is silent and is found to be wise;
another is hated for his endless chatter.
One man is silent, at a loss for an answer;
another is silent, biding his time.
The wise man is silent until the right moment,
but a swaggering fool is always speaking out of turn.
A garrulous man makes himself detested,
and one who abuses his position arouses hatred
(Ecclesiasticus [Sirach] 4:23-26, 5:11-14, 11:8, 20:5-8).

The wise man Sirach shares with us these lucid observations and rules for dialogue. The art of dialogue plays a necessary role in securing harmony on the path of truth. He emphasizes especially the discernment of participants, the readiness to listen and to learn, and the need for mutual support in the search for wisdom.

There is an unchangeable relationship between our dialogue with God and our dialogue with fellow human beings. In communion with God it is evident that the first condition is to listen and to acknowledge God's initiative. He speaks to us through all his creation, through the events of our lives and our times, and — in a special way — through people who have opened themselves to his wisdom and kindness. Happy are those who live with others who know how to listen to God and to make all their life a response to him!

Jesus Christ is not only the final and supreme Word spoken to us by the Father; he is also the matchless master of dialogue. The incarnate Son lives wholly by the word that comes from the Father. He is the perfect listener.

To Israel, chosen to be his servant and messenger, God says:

Hear now, you that are deaf;
you blind men, look and see:
yet who is blind but my servant,
who so deaf as the messenger whom I send? . . . (Isaiah 42:18-19)

But of the new Israel, the Servant, it is foretold:

The Lord GOD has given me
the tongue of a teacher
and skill to console the weary . . .
he sharpened my hearing
that I might listen like one who is taught.
The Lord GOD opened my ears
and I did not disobey . . . (Isaiah 50:4-5).

The Gospel shows us clearly how strikingly Jesus has listened to the words of God in the Holy Scriptures but equally how attentively he listens to wise people, to the needs of people, and to the cry of the downtrodden and sinners.

18

Jesus, the teacher, dialogues with his friends and also with his enemies. By listening he receives the information he wants. He asks questions and responds to questions. Through dialogue he learns what others are experiencing and the problems they are facing; and from there he leads them patiently to a deeper vision. What a wonderful example is his dialogue with the woman of Samaria! (See John, chapter 4.)

Dialogue is a basic human experience. It becomes an excellent form of human art when people not only speak words with each other but also express themselves in openness and trust, manifesting their love and assuring each other of their fidelity.

Dialogue in Marriage

The quality, stability, and happiness of a marriage depend greatly on the quality of the dialogue between spouses. In a good married and family life, behind all the words and gestures stands the basic communication: "It is good that you *are*! It is good that I can *be* for you!" Authentic conjugal love in all its dimensions, but especially in the conjugal embrace, is that wonderful dialogue in which the spouses open their hearts to each other and entrust themselves to each other.

Good partners, gifted with the art of dialogue, do not pick words apart, as untender hands sometimes do to flowers, nor do they just listen to words. They meet their partners as unique persons, with an intuitive sense of the kindness, happiness, sympathy, trouble, or pain which underlies the other's words and gestures.

In its full sense, dialogue is sharing joy and sorrow with the other; it is grateful reception and enrichment not only of knowledge and experience but also of learning to love better, with greater sympathy and reverence, and thus also to discover each other's inner being and resources.

The effect of dialogue depends on both its content and the way it is conducted. A marriage or friendship gains much if, in the partners' dialogue, there is a sharing of high ideals, vital interests, commitment to an important cause, and a continuing search for deeper knowledge of truth and wisdom.

Dialogue between spouses and between teachers and children can bear rich fruit in the field of education. Happy are the children whose parents and educators are masters of dialogue, willing and able to listen to the children in their uniqueness, joys, and needs, and to speak with them in such a way that they can better discover their capabilities and meet their difficulties!

Children can help us to progress in the art of dialogue and to understand what Jesus meant when he invited us to become like children, single-minded, cordial, open. The child experiences great encouragement when his or her first efforts to talk are taken seriously and are a source of joy for the family. But long before children articulate words and sentences they have begun a kind of dialogue; they are already communicating effectively in many ways their joy, fear, pain, attachment, hunger, and need for love.

If parents and educators are competent partners in dialogue, children will express themselves confidently in conversation and questions. When parents acknowledge that they do not know the right answer to a question and need time to think about it, the child begins to learn an important aspect of good dialogue. And it is even more fruitful for the child's education — as well as for all participants in the dialogue — if a parent confesses with truthful simplicity, "I was wrong; I should not have said (or done) that; I am sorry."

Not the least of dialogue's riches are sharing joy with the other and being open to the various forms of enjoyment. For this a sense of humor can be a marvelous charism. Serious discussions need to be enlivened from time to time with a humorous story or a bit of wit; and even in a time of sadness the conversation needs to be lightened with moments of cheer, of hope, of happy or humorous reminiscences. And all these can be offered by the Christian without coming down from the Mount of the Beatitudes.

Sirach calls our attention to the art of listening, of silence — alertness for the right moment and the right word. To learn all this takes time and patience. We have to examine the quality of our dialogue again and again in order to improve it. Among friends, and especially between spouses, it might be advisable or at times necessary to have a heart-to-heart talk about the meaning, purpose, and quality of their day-by-day dialogue.

Dialogue is expression of our complementarity. In a mature dialogue we acknowledge the other as other, and are grateful that he or she is different from us. This is particularly important in the dialogue between man and woman. It can be enriching only if both affirm, by word and deed, their equal dignity and rejoice in their diversity.

Dialogue between (among) all concerned parties is the proper way to arrive at decisions. One of the greatest evils in today's world is the arrogance of individuals and groups who set themselves up as sole arbiters of the economic, cultural, and political matters which deeply affect the lives of others. The decisions would be more fair and more prudent if all concerned were allowed to contribute their skills, experiences, viewpoints, and interests. It would then also be much easier to put decisions into practice.

Patient and respectful dialogue in the search for truth and for meaningful solutions to common problems is at the heart of the sharing family. The dignity of all members is thus constantly reaffirmed, and the children gradually learn to accept more and more responsibility. Ultimately, the quality of dialogue on the family level will determine whether the high ideals of democracy in the social, cultural, and political realms will actually be of service to genuine human development and peace.

Dialogue with the World

To share or communicate faith by witness and word in marriage, family, among friends, in prayer groups, and in direct pastoral activities is one of the noblest forms of dialogue. At the heart of this dialogue lies our common effort to discern events and experiences in the light of faith. In this way we share the joy of faith and the consolation that comes from God and leads to him.

The dialogue of faith becomes perfect when the participants are aware that they are gathered in the name of the Lord and he is present with them. Ideal friendship is anchored in this friendship with the Lord. The dialogue between believing friends arises from and leads to the intimate dialogue with the Lord.

Paul's first Letter to the Corinthians (especially chapter 14) shows us how spontaneous and dynamic the dialogue of faith was in that early community. Because of these characteristics, efforts had to be made to keep it on a high level and at the same time to guarantee a minimum of order. The saint's letters indicate also that in the dialogue of faith a great diversity of charisms and experiences were included. The belief that this diversity enriched dialogue and unity was grounded in the truth that the *one* Spirit builds up unity through the very diversity of gifts and ministries, since each charism is given by the Spirit for the benefit of all.

The Letter to the Philippians, in which Paul, prisoner for the Lord's sake, gives consolation and exhortation, also lays down the basic rules for dialogue. "If then our common life in Christ yields anything to stir the heart, any loving consolation, any sharing of the Spirit, any warmth of affection or compassion, fill up my cup of happiness by thinking and feeling alike, with the same love for one another, the same turn of mind, and a common care for unity. There must be no room for rivalry and personal vanity among you, but you must humbly reckon others better than yourselves. Look to each other's interest and not merely to your own" (Philippians 2:1-4).

What Paul prescribes for the individual is also true for the entire Church. Those in authority depend greatly on the manifold charisms and particular skills available among the People of God. All this needs encouragement and the kind of channeling which favors creativity and produces results for the benefit of all.

The basic principles of collegiality and subsidiarity point in this direction. In the worldwide Catholic Church there must be ample room, even on the institutional level, for dialogue among the various cultures, historical experiences, traditions, customs, skills, and needs. A fanaticism for uniformity is an impoverishment and an enemy of love and mutual appreciation.

If the Church, in her inner life, shows herself as a model of fostering and articulating dialogue on all levels, then she can also make a most valuable contribution to the promotion of dialogue within the secular world — between social classes, ethnic groups, cultures and subcultures, political parties, and even among the various ideologies and world views. No one can doubt that the art of dialogue is a basic premise for all endeavors to bring about peace and justice.

Prayer

Lord, how exciting it is to know that all of your creation and all the events of redemption originated in a dialogue with us. You made us capable of listening, and you assure us that you are interested in our response. In all our needs, as well as in our joys, we are encouraged to speak to you with gratitude and confidence.

Lord, teach us how to be silent before you in order to understand better your message. Speak to our hearts as well as to our minds. Move our wills so that we can entrust ourselves to you and always search earnestly to understand your design for us.

We thank you, loving Father, for the gift of speech and language, for ears and tongue. We thank you for all the loving people who share with us not only their knowledge but also the art of loving, the art of listening to console and to encourage.

Lord, send forth your Spirit to teach us to remain open to that dialogue which makes each one of us an image and likeness of your triune life and of your loving presence among us. Teach us the kind of prayer that nourishes fruitful human dialogue, responds to your initiative, and foreshadows the divine dialogue of heaven. We praise forever your bounty which invites us even now to be adorers of your divine life in word and love.

3
REJOICE IN GOD'S CREATED BEAUTY

So in the Spirit he carried me away to a great high mountain, and showed me the holy city of Jerusalem coming down out of heaven from God. It shone with the glory of God; it had the radiance of some priceless jewel, like a jasper, clear as crystal. It had a great high wall. . . . The wall was built of jasper, while the city itself was of pure gold, bright as clear glass. The foundations of the city wall were adorned with jewels of every kind, the first of the foundation-stones being jasper, the second lapis lazuli, the third chalcedony, the fourth emerald, the fifth sardonyx, the sixth cornelian, the seventh chryso-lite, the eighth beryl, the ninth topaz, the tenth chrysoprase, the eleventh turquoise, and the twelfth amethyst. The twelve gates were twelve pearls, each gate being made from a single pearl. The streets of the city were made of pure gold, like translucent glass (Revelations 21:10-11,18-21).

The face of holiness is not repulsive. If the all-holy God draws us totally to himself in order to make us a shining light for the world, he does so by the splendor of his bounty, his bliss, and the attractive power of all the beauty he has revealed. To rejoice in beauty is an essential dimension of humanness. If this is absent or inactive, there is no way we can approach the morality of the Beatitudes and the praise of God's glory.

Someone brought a beautiful bouquet of flowers to the sickbed of a man who was addicted to eating and drinking too much. He did not even look at them but curtly asked the nurse to take them away, saying: "What good are these flowers? I can't eat or drink them!"

Of course, there is nothing wrong with enjoying good food and wine, which are also God's gifts, foreshadowing the heavenly feast and remindful of the Eucharistic meal; but how could one imagine the joyous banquet with God and all his saints if one's pleasure is restricted to what one can eat or drink? How wretched is the person who cannot rejoice in beauty, bounty, signs of friendship, who cannot admire and be grateful for what is good, true, and beautiful in itself! Nothing is left to such a one but hangovers and boredom.

Our sick man, who sees no meaning in beautiful flowers, was probably — in his healthy days — a great achiever and a hard worker, even boastful of his sense of duty. He is representative of a substantial part of our society which, despite its highly organized leisure-time activities, is appallingly empty: lacking esthetic feeling, without appreciation for music, wanting in religious dimension, with no taste for the good news coming from God and leading to him, no appetite for an enthusiastic faith or for gratitude and praise to God.

God did not create and redeem his world for mere consumption and production. Utility is not the prime motivation for men and women and the creation entrusted to them. The biblical account of creation evokes words of marvel and admiration; it elicits joy, thanksgiving, praise. To rejoice in something that is beautiful, without worrying whether it is useful, is a wonderful act of gratitude to God.

What Beauty Says to Us

According to Saint Thomas Aquinas, beauty is one of the most characteristic names of God. Creation and redemption are revelation of his glory, splendor of his own beauty. The vision in the Book of Revelation quoted at the beginning of this chapter is an essential feature of God's promises. It presumes our taste for beauty.

Beauty speaks to us in our wholeness; it is attractive beyond all considerations of utility and profit. Loving people — beautiful and attractive themselves — discover the beauty, the goodness, the authenticity of others. They see others' inner resources and summon them to life. Openness to beauty unfolds in contemplation and is a most pleasant way to reach all that is good and true. Indeed, beauty itself is the splendor of what is true and good.

Whoever has developed an appreciation for authentic beauty cannot be seduced by cheap sex appeal; such a person will seek out people who beautifully radiate truthfulness, kindness, serenity, peace. One senses that these people are of themselves an invitation to strive for goodness and authenticity.

In its enchanting purity and integrity, beauty speaks to the believer with an inner language that sings of the glory of a loving Creator who, in all his works, reveals his own beauty and generosity. Saint Augustine expresses a primary religious experience of millions of people when he prays: "How beautiful is everything which you have made! But how ineffably more beautiful are you, the Creator of all things!"

Beauty and Glory

The Holy Spirit is called not only the Spirit of Truth but also the "glorious Spirit" (1 Peter 4:14). Whoever is guided by the Spirit in a life of constant gratitude and grateful service is led to an ever deeper and more blessed knowledge of the "Father of glory," the "Lord of glory and majesty."

The word "glory" is a key word in Holy Scripture. Religious people speak of glory when they are wholly seized by God's attractive and awe-inspiring majesty, filled with joy by his nearness and love, and by a fervent fear in the face of his holiness.

This basic experience of holy fear, of awe, marvel, and bliss, gives to the Christian the strength to follow Christ crucified, in view of "the revelation of the glory of God in the face of Jesus Christ" (2 Corinthians 4:6), for Jesus "caused his light to shine within us."

When he is ready to drink the bitter chalice and to accept the outrage of the Cross, Jesus prays to the Father: "The glory which thou gavest me I have given to them, that they may be one, as we are one. . . . Father, I desire that these men, who are thy gift to me, may be with me where I am, so that they may look upon my glory, which thou hast given me because thou didst love me before the world began" (John 17:22-24). A Christian cannot think about everlasting happiness without constantly praising God's glory and majesty, as well as marveling at his attractive and awe-inspiring beauty — that beauty whose blissful and resplendent rays already light the faces of saints.

The biblical morality of the Beatitudes is a morality of beauty and glory, infinitely more fruitful and attractive than a mere morality of duties and prohibitions. Those who develop the sense of beauty gain a better access and a more grateful relationship to the whole of reality. Experiencing the boundless beauty of God's good world, they open themselves wholly to a morality of grace and graciousness. They sense then the depth of the words of Saint Paul: "You are no longer under law, but under the grace of God" (Romans 6:14).

The Gift of Beauty

An inner relationship with beauty, in view of him who *is* Beauty, gives to the Christian life a note of joy, courage, and creativity. Beauty itself is a gratuitous gift. It does not cry "do this, do that," but it transforms the human mind and heart, intuition, spirit, and will. It forms a personality whose relationship with the realm of the good, the honest, the fitting, and the truth is inborn: a Christian person who finds his or her joy in God.

This is shown in the lives of the saints. We think of Saint Francis of Assisi and his joy in whatever is beautiful, especially the simple and ordinary things. This allowed him a kind of espousal with "Lady Poverty" in a constant festival of joy. Or we think of Saint Alphonsus, so enraptured by the beauty of divine love and glory that in the midst of a sermon he could compose songs and sing the good news into the hearts of the faithful: songs which for hundreds of years have reechoed his enthusiasm for the Emmanuel — God with us. Some of his spiritual works, for instance *The Art of Loving Jesus Christ*, have awakened enthusiasm in thousands of readers.

So now, as always, the world needs saints who will educate children, youth, and adults to appreciate beauty as it radiates the good and the true. This is an absolute necessity if we want to help our culture to rise above an insensitive, sterile, consumer-producer mentality. Such a growth would also do much for the liberation of our society from the ugliness of aggressiveness and violence.

Everyone is meant by God to become a masterpiece of his love and, at the same time, his co-artist in his wonderful work of forming human beings in his authentic image. Everyone can develop some dimension of art, of creativity. But whatever our individual skills or limits in human arts, we can become masters in the supreme art of being loving and lovable people — indeed, of becoming saints and helping each other in this most wonderful art. We have the divine promises. What the world needs now is not so much producers or consumers of mass-produced goods; it needs beautiful, whole, and holy people.

Prayer

Father of glory and majesty, we praise you for all the beauty of your creation: the bright firmament, the green of our meadows, the quiet and healthy air of the forests, the gaiety and splendor of flowers, the love songs of birds, and the ever-new beauty of myriad species of animals. Wherever we look, we see the reflection of your own beauty, inviting us to marvel, to admire, to praise, and to thank you.

We praise you for each smile of a beloved child, for the radiant faces of true lovers, for the hope-inspiring beauty of mature graciousness in so many people, for the magnificent wholeness of holy people.

We praise you for your wonders in the history of salvation, for the Book of Psalms, and all the Holy Scriptures, which teach us to discover ever better the beauty of all your works and the admirable wisdom revealed in the work of redemption.

Above all, we praise you for the great miracle of the Incarnation of your beloved Son, Jesus Christ, for his gracious kindness to all who came to him, for the majesty of his forgiveness and love on the Cross, for the revelation of your glory in his Resurrection, and for the promise of our resurrection in glory if our life here on earth glorifies your majesty and love.

Lord, teach us to marvel, to admire, to praise, and to thank you for your beauty and the beauty of all your creation.

4

HARMONIZE LABOR
WITH LEISURE

I rejoiced when they said to me,
  'Let us go to the house of the LORD.'
Now we stand within your gates,
  O Jerusalem:
Jerusalem that is built to be a city
  where people come together in unity;
to which the tribes resort, the tribes of the LORD,
  to give thanks to the LORD himself,
  the bounden duty of Israel.
For in her are set the thrones of justice,
  the thrones of the house of David.
Pray for the peace of Jerusalem:
  'May those who love you prosper;
peace be within your ramparts
  and prosperity in your palaces.'
For the sake of these my brothers and my friends,
  I will say, 'Peace be within you.'
For the sake of the house of the LORD our God
  I will pray for your good (Psalm 122).

Frequently, I have heard the following description of the difference between typical Germans and typical Italians: ''Germans live to work; Italians work to live.'' If this is true, the Italians are winning the match — provided, however, they know the art of living.

The ultimate meaning of life lies neither in work nor in play. A fulfilled life implies both meaningful leisure and honorable, socially relevant work. In the biblical sense life is, above all, a feast manifesting its meaning and joy in all of life's dimensions.

Jesus has not only labored in our behalf and borne the burden of the Cross; we know him equally as the one who concelebrated the feasts of Israel, sang the joyful songs of the pilgrims on their way to the house of God. He exulted in his work and his praise of his Father. These were his resources which gave him the strength to carry his Cross. Before he went up to the Mount of Olives and to Mount Calvary he instituted the Eucharist which anticipates and leads us to the heavenly banquet of eternal bliss.

Being a Christian surely requires the readiness to follow Christ, the crucified; but it also means that we are set free for joyous festival, dancing before the Lord, quiet contemplation, raptures of love, conviviality, laughter flowing from a liberating sense of humor.

Festive and leisure time constitute a relaxed but firm *yes* to life's meaning, an occasion for sharing life's joys, strengthening solidarity in joy and sorrow, and developing creativity. All this has great impact on our personal growth, creative liberty, and fidelity.

A Sense of Celebration

If we celebrate feast days and make our life festive in expectation of the eternal feast, then we know that life is good, that it is wonderful to live together, that life has an ultimate purpose beyond all the purposes of organized work. We have every reason for contemplation and celebration. We are constantly being invited to rejoice in all that is good, true, and beautiful as we recall our roots which come from God who is love, goodness, truth, bliss.

Quite different are the festive occasions and leisure times of persons driven by the anguish of not being able to amass enough material goods to satisfy themselves. The prophet gives us a sad

31

picture of them: "Let us eat and drink; for tomorrow we die" (Isaiah 22:13). They resort to the loudest music in an effort to still the outcry of the poor and the cry of their own hearts which yearn for ultimate meaning, true love, and joy. They hope that incessant noise will deafen them to their inner voice that calls for conversion.

Even more deplorable are the "festivals" of the dictators whose ideologies call for a class struggle to free the masses but who, in their lust for power, their deadly bureaucracy, and their murderous arms race, have already buried even the false hopes of their original ideology. So they feast on the great parades of their newest weaponry and the applause of their propagandized masses.

Leisure, festive celebration, play, and dance mean more than repose from work and restoration of strength for work. They bear meaning in themselves for all who are searching for life's final meaning. They are gateways to new horizons.

The Book of Genesis helps us to discover the meaning of the Sabbath in view of the supreme dignity of humankind, created in God's own image. The seventh day should remind God's people not only of the Creator's works but also of his repose, his celebration of love and joy, over and above all his works (see Genesis 1:27; 2:1-4).

God does not want us to be drudges, slaves of work. The holy days guaranteeing repose and leisure are meant to help us develop our noblest capacities for worship, for joy, and for love. Only thus can we be faithful and creative stewards of the earth entrusted to us. No one can be a true image of God in work unless he or she is first of all his image in the festive joy that calls for love and unity.

Jesus insists that the Sabbath is for people (see Mark 2:27). It is a privilege, an invitation to a supreme sharing in God's feast day of peace, but it is also a fundamental social rule to protect servants, migrants, slaves (see Exodus 20:10). It reminds everyone that, before God, the poor and oppressed are of the same dignity as the rich and powerful, and that no one may celebrate the feast of liberation wrought by God while refusing to others who are weaker a share in the benefits. The world — economic, cultural, social, and political

— needs saints who celebrate life in this way, as a feast to which all others are invited.

Joy in the Liturgy

Our Christian life is marked by the year's liturgical cycle. The feast days of the year and the Christian Sunday offer a sharing in salvation history through grateful remembrance of God's wonderful deeds of creation and redemption, the expectation of an eternal sharing in God's glory and bliss, and the ongoing discovery of present opportunities.

Festive and leisure time do not lull Christians to sleep or to forgetfulness of injustice and misery in the world. Rather, those who truly celebrate the feasts of salvation are encouraged not only to deal with their own troubles but also to bear the burdens of others. They know well that only in this way will they celebrate with all those of good will the feast of eternal life.

The Eucharist, sacrifice and banquet, memorial and pledge of abiding hope, opens our eyes to the abyss of sin in the light of Christ's Cross, but also assures us of the final victory of justice and love. Our celebration of the remembrance and hope of liberation, and of the presence of God who is the helper of the poor, is sincere and productive only if we unite with others in the struggle for the dignity and liberty of all people.

Some persons seem to think that their serious commitment to social and political action allows or even commands them to ignore feast and worship. They are wrong. They deny themselves the very inner resources of peace, without which they cannot prevent discord, hatred, or injustice. If we refuse to take time to adore God in community and to welcome his Good News, we miss the chance to exorcise the false gods from our own hearts and the dangerous idols from public life.

The calendar of Christian feast days and the regular observance of Sunday (which repeatedly celebrates the Easter event) is an amazing gift from the Lord of salvation history. It is also a pedagogical masterpiece. Humankind would not be so restless and unstable if it would thankfully accept this divine pedagogy. Not all the sporting events at stadiums or entertainment at the theater or on television will fill the void in the souls and lives of those who reject the rhythm of the Christian feast days and Sundays; entertainment in excess serves to alienate the viewer from festive celebration.

This does not imply that the feast days and celebrations of the Church claim a kind of monopoly. But their centrality touches on all the joys and sorrows of life, yet leaves room for the myriad forms of festivity and recreation. And everything that is genuine in the festive celebrations of families, neighborhoods, and cultures, can serve as a prelude to the religious celebrations.

Holy people are not killjoys. The dimension of dance and play is indispensable in human culture. The child needs play, playmates, and joy in play. Parents who play with their children reap their own joyous harvest of serenity. Delight in play and regard for the rules of fair play prevent a too heavy seriousness and allow participants to work together as a team in preparation for future tasks in life.

As if in an enchanting playlet, Holy Scripture tells us of the working of divine wisdom and of the invitation to the feast which divine wisdom prepares for those whom she loves (see Proverbs 9:1-6). And she says further:

> Then I was at his side each day,
> his darling and delight,
> playing in his presence continually,
> playing on the earth, when he had finished it,
> while my delight was in mankind (Proverbs 8:30-31).

On the way to the eternal feast in the glory of God, we are team players, "members of the cast" in the tremendous play of redemption, of the gradual breakthrough of joy and love.

Surely, we also need purposefulness in our life, a prudent coordination of means (tools and methods) and ends (goals). But goals and tools must not be allowed to dominate us. God offers us many joys without subordinating them in any way to direct purposes. We should habitually accept the invitation simply to rejoice, to sing, and to play!

A Sense of Humor

Throughout history, artists in various fields have portrayed human beings as echoes of God's rejoicing in his creation and redemption. If the objection is made that we are far from being "simply redeemed," then I suggest that there is even a greater need for play therapy, the joy of team play, for wit and humor. Christians who know that they are redeemed can laugh in spite of all their problems, in spite of all their misery; for they believe that the last word in history is the victory of love and joy.

Not all Christians, not even all saintly persons, are especially gifted with a sense of humor; but no saint will ever disdain this wonderful gift. It is, indeed, a priceless charism that often provides proper perspective for the discussion at hand, and opens our eyes to a more balanced vision of what is happening. It can be a marvelous peacemaking charism. As Christians, we recognize the world's natural inclination to evil; we know about folly and sin. But we also know that, after all, victory lies in plentiful redemption. So we allow ourselves and others a touch of levity while constantly striving for greater wisdom.

A genuine and healthy sense of humor never focuses on other people's faults or foibles. The tone and target of our humor should rest on the constant awareness that we, too, have our faults. We all need the therapy which humor provides.

Christian humor has its roots in the knowledge that, in spite of our sins and shortcomings, we are accepted and reconciled by God. Our *yes* to God arises from our firm hope in final salvation. An uplifting and agreeable sense of humor is a concrete sign and symbol of faith that conquers the hearts of many; it originates not from superficial or blind optimism but from actual contact with God's graciousness, which allows us to discover a reason for wit and laughter where others see only doom. It signals hope and redeemed freedom.

Prayer

We thank you, Father, that on our pilgrimage you grant us not only time to rest after all our toil but also festive joy and leisure for contemplation. Like children, we can play before you, confident that it pleases you to see us bring happiness to each other by playing together and celebrating in community.

We thank you for the great feast days of the Church in which we can experience salvation solidarity and shared joy. Through them you remind us of our past salvation history and direct our eyes and steps toward the eternal homeland. You help us, too, to discover the richness of the present moment, reassuring us of your abiding presence and loving care.

I thank you, Lord, for the yearly remembrance of my birthday and day of Baptism. You have called me into being, given me a unique name, and have assumed me into the family of the redeemed.

I thank you for all my family's feasts and celebrations, for play and song with brothers and sisters, for the time my parents took to play and to talk with me.

Thank you, Father, for the wonderful people who, through wit and humor, have helped us to see redemption at work and to discover essential dimensions of life, of beauty, of inner liberty and creativity.

Grant that, for all of us, feast, dance and play, song and sense of humor may be part of our grateful experience of your redemption at work.

Free the world from all vicious resolve and cold calculation which often lead to tensions and war. Teach us to announce to the world your vision of liberation!

5
CHALLENGE THE MASS MEDIA

The heavens tell out the glory of God,
the vault of heaven reveals his handiwork.
One day speaks to another,
night with night shares its knowledge,
    and this without speech or language
    or sound of any voice.
Their music goes out through all the earth,
    their words reach to the end of the world (Psalm 19:1-4).

There is nothing covered up that will not be uncovered, nothing
hidden that will not be made known. What I say to you in the dark
you must repeat in broad daylight; what you hear whispered you
must shout from the house-tops (Matthew 10:26-27).

Few matters challenge the Christian's discernment and talent as
much as the modern mass media. If Christians who excel in this field
can transmit to it strong convictions, the art of dialogue, vigilance for
the signs of the times, and discernment, then they are the kind of
people this world urgently needs today.

Modern mass media offer a unique opportunity for proclaiming the
Good News literally "from the housetops" — think of all those TV
aerials! The potential of the various forms of news, information, and
entertainment media is stupendous. They can remind us of our moral
obligations to solve the urgent problems of our times; they can spread
peace-fostering information, give voice to the voiceless, awaken
people's consciences about the hungry, the exploited, the victims of

catastrophies; and they can be instrumental in organizing actions of solidarity from one end of the earth to the other.

On the other hand, there is nothing more dangerous than the same mass media in the hands of the unscrupulous, the enforcers of subversive ideologies, or exploiters of human passion, greed, and aggression. The infatuation of a great portion of the German population with Hitler exemplifies this; for it could hardly have been possible without a shrewd use of the radio to propagandize a people not yet prepared for discernment in its use.

When Hitler came to power each family was offered a receiver at almost no cost. My own father's reaction was sharp: ''As long as this man is in power, no receiver will come into our house; I don't want his voice heard in our home!'' A neighboring family, as devout and Church-oriented as ours, took the receiver. After a few years they had not, thank God, lost their faith, but their trust in the Church leaders was undermined, and many of Hitler's slogans had taken over a good part of their thinking and their language.

Some years later — while I was in Russia — I found homes equipped with radio loudspeakers which could not be turned off and whose programs could not be personally selected. They had been designed and placed there by the Stalinists. Both of these regimes threatened grave sanctions against anyone who would dare to listen to another country's radio lest they absorb its ''subversive'' ideology.

Ways to Challenge

Development of the mass media has brought and is still bringing forth profound cultural and psychological changes. This is a field where Christians should make their presence known in many ways: not only through token religious programs but in all areas, especially the cultural and entertainment fields. We have to be well informed about how the mass media shape human consciousness; and we must learn how to use them, avoiding every kind of mind manipulation, while promoting the values of critical appreciation, creative liberty, and constructive action.

Those who are interested in the development of humanity will use all possible means to influence the media in this regard. But to do so they must learn to judge their own reaction fairly and begin to cultivate intensively the virtue of discernment.

When letterpress printing appeared some five hundred years ago and began to exercise a growing influence on public opinion, the Church reacted one-sidedly, using all available means of control, censure, and sanction. The index of forbidden books was one of its measures. This was understandable, since the public was in no way prepared to use necessary discernment. Of course, this kind of repressive control over the modern mass media (radio, movies, TV) is absolutely impossible now, and most people react negatively to control systems. But responsible users of the media can praise good programs, recommend certain movies and plays, and warn against error and decadence. However, a warning in the form of loud condemnation by Church authorities can become a boomerang and sometimes make an otherwise unsuccessful book, movie, or play a money-maker.

What really matters today is that each individual, family, group, and community try to grow in discernment and foster the same in Church and society. Person-to-person promotion of good books, periodicals, movies, TV programs, and the like is a very effective means of promoting the good and increasing one's own competence in discernment. Shared efforts in such actions are especially effective.

In this area, too, we should not forget one of the basic Christian and human principles: Look first to discovering and promoting the good. Then we can also more systematically and effectively face the evil, unmask deceptions and dangers, and warn against them.

The modern mass media provide a new opportunity for all social classes and all nations with easier access to our common cultural heritage. But a concerted effort is needed to guarantee a certain moral and cultural level, to check the efforts of power cliques in their abuse of the media, and to block effectively any kind of group monopoly.

This is one of the most important fields for the exercise of the lay apostolate and the pursuit of professional excellence.

A serious danger here is passive reception, exposing oneself uncritically to a haphazard stream of news and entertainment without asking what good or harm is presented, how credible and how relevant are the various programs, and what kind of action is provoked. Another danger is the exaggerated cult of the stars in literary and entertainment fields and even in the sports world, which cult often leads to the imitation of those who least deserve it. Many people tend to accept opinions uncritically simply because they are uttered by their favorite stars.

Other Means of Influence

The media customer, if competent in a given area, should be active in many ways. Active participation in pertinent dialogue allows one to exercise a beneficial influence on public opinion instead of exposing oneself defenselessly to all kinds of dubious influences.

The simplest means of influence is by judicious choice of the products provided by the press, films, cassettes, radio and TV programs; in this way the client speaks forcefully through the market itself. Another important means is by letters to the editor, journalist, or artist, especially if it is a competent expression given with a constructive attitude. It is not fitting, however, to send only letters of censure and reproach. The constant carper quickly loses any chance of being listened to or taken seriously. Positive appraisal, however, can be very effective.

The director of a broadcasting company once told me that, frequently, good programs, good music, and good entertainment have little chance because nobody requests them and nobody praises them. Many years ago, when I was still teaching in our seminary in Germany, I was visited by a friend of a famous entertainer who had died a few days before. He had come to bring to our students the entertainer's greetings uttered on his deathbed. Some weeks previously they had written a collective letter to him, praising his combination of good taste, expertise, and propriety. His reaction had been one of great joy; but he also remarked: "During so many years of my career I never received any acknowledgment from any churchman; yet what these students of theology have praised in my work was my most serious concern during my whole life."

Families should give serious attention to the choice of TV programs, since this means inviting guests into their home and recommending them to their children. The adults, adolescents, and children should meet frequently in a common effort to make good choices. If they first discuss the criteria and then exchange their evaluations after having watched the programs, they will be sure that it is they, and not their TV guests, who have the last word in their home. But, unfortunately, in many families the art of dialogue and even common family prayer have been silenced by the craving for ever-new programs which are received uncritically and passively.

Discipline Needed

The consumer of mass media products needs many forms of self-discipline. It is not sufficient to protect oneself against vicious and noxious quality. Quantity, too, has to be examined. How much time is spent in watching? How many frivolous impressions have been made? How much money is spent in operating the set? How much passivity is created in the children?

Those who realize how much the audio-visual media influence and change our psychic life need no further admonition. But those who continue to overuse the mass media and react too passively to its influence will become addicted consumers with no ability to assimilate the material presented. Such people gradually lose the contemplative dimensions of life. The art of dialogue becomes even more difficult and more rare.

Years ago I was invited by a group of Major Superiors to a study week on the problems of chastity in religious life. Also present were some outstanding psychologists and psychotherapists. I was amazed when I heard a well-known psychologist from Harvard University, the mother of several children, suggest to the Superiors that they advise their confreres to abstain from TV and movies for perhaps a year and then assess their first reactions when watching again what they had earlier watched so often. She also pointed out that, on television and in magazines, the blatant use of sex appeal to sell products causes the passive receiver of these messages to eventually draw the conclusion that sexuality is just another article of consumption.

This leads us to another dimension of a much-needed form of self-discipline for those who expose themselves too often to TV publicity and advertisement. Their "new commandments" are: "Thou shalt covet; thou shalt buy more things; thou shalt consume more. . . . " We have to be on guard against these "hidden seducers."

Particularly dangerous is the intensive advertisement for psychotropic drugs. By word and picture the uncritical watcher is lulled into the belief that almost all troublesome emotions, stresses, and pains can be relieved by taking the recommended drug. The drug addiction in our society is only the tip of the iceberg of an ever-growing tendency — propagated by the drug industry — to take psychotropic pills instead of recognizing and organizing one's own spiritual and psychological resources, living within one's capacities, and cherishing healthier relationships with one's family, neighbors, and community.

Through the modern mass media, almost everyone today is either passively exposed to or has perceptively understood the pluralism of cultures and world views. The era of closed groups and cultures has ended. People are no longer guided by uniform traditions, customs, mores, world views, convictions. The media allows us to compare these dimensions in all their diversity.

This can be taken as a challenge to search more thoroughly for truth and solid moral convictions, and thereby to sink deeper roots into the community of faith. There one finds the most authentic help, especially when it fosters careful discernment and distinction between abiding truth of divine revelation on one hand and changing human traditions and world views on the other.

The need for mature discernment is heightened by the fact that today's pluralism places constructive dialogue and peaceful discussion in competition with intolerant and aggressive ideologies, as well as economic and political systems whose weaponry is the ruthless manipulation of people's minds.

Unfortunately, many Christians are not prepared to confront the complex problem of pluralism critically and constructively. We all should help one another to hold firmly to the abiding truths and principles of our faith and to unmask dangerous errors. At the same time we should remain open-minded to the great diversity of life expressions, which can be vital personifications of the one faith in various times and cultures. For this, too, the world needs persons who live the Gospel: mature and competent Christians.

The manner in which Christians are present in the area of the mass media will determine how much influence they will have in deciding the burning questions of our day and our world, such as the reconciliation of the Christian churches and harmony and peace among nations.

Prayer

God, our Father, we adore you for the wonders of your revelation. We thank you for Christ, the great communicator on earth. We praise you for sending us the Spirit of Truth, enabling us to become attentive receivers and skillful and reverent communicators of truth.

We praise you, God, for having enabled men and women to discover ever more the secrets hidden in your creation, allowing them to communicate by radio, telegraphy, television, and new satellite systems, so that news can go from one end of the earth to the other in seconds. We are grateful for this progress in research which tells us of ever-new dimensions of the greatness of your creation.

Father, we do believe that it is your design to lead us all to you through your communication in creation and redemption. We thank you for the mass media, through which you invite the whole of humanity to a worldwide dialogue, new forms of solidarity, and new means of fostering peace. Help us, Lord, to reach that level of wisdom and discernment that allows us to make beneficial use of all these means.

6
SHAPE PUBLIC OPINION

Shame on you! you who drag wickedness along like a tethered sheep,
  and sin like a heifer on a rope. . . .
Shame on you! you who call evil good and good evil,
who turn darkness into light and light into darkness,
who make bitter sweet and sweet bitter.
  Shame on you! you who are wise in your own eyes
    and prudent in your own esteem (Isaiah 5:18,20-21).

Since living a Christian life means essentially mission to be "light to the world," it is unthinkable that a genuine Christian would ignore or neglect his or her share of responsibility for the formation of healthy public opinion in the surrounding environment and in society at large. A joint effort to enlighten and shape public opinion is a basic function of our care for the common good.

Of course, I do not speak here of merely theoretical opinions which have no relevance for life, love, and justice in human relationships. Rather, I have in mind those convictions and opinions which shape the human milieu, human encounter and cooperation, individual and collective responsibility.

Public Opinion

Here are some examples that will explain my meaning. Public opinion on one burning issue of the day may say, "Life is something wonderful, a sign of God's creative presence. Human life, from the very beginning, is entrusted to the responsibility and protection of all.

If society and state do not protect the life of the weakest and most innocent ones, the common good is shaken at its very foundations.'' But in some circles, public opinion may sound like this: ''My womb is mine. Therefore it's nobody else's business if I interrupt my unwanted pregnancy.''

In the economic realm, one camp of public opinion tells us: ''What counts in the national economy is the quantitative growth of output. If a government fails in this area, it should be turned out.'' Yet I am convinced that I should influence public opinion by taking a different tact, since I believe that the struggle for ever more output and the tendency to measure prosperity and the common good by the quantitative national gross product are grievous errors leading to disastrous consequences for the future and dignity of humankind. This mania for quantitative growth can gravely harm the authentic whole-person growth of ourselves and our communities. If we do not free ourselves from this ''more, more,'' ''bigger, bigger'' madness, then sooner or later it will lead to a worldwide conflict, and even to an ecological collapse.

A third example is equally pressing. One group, focusing on the question of human health, insists on the right of health care for all. ''The state and society have to do much more for health, and I have the right to get as much as possible from them and from my insurance policies.'' But again I choose to think differently. Certainly the common good and justice require our state and society (we ourselves) to provide the best possible care for the sick, the handicapped, and the poor. But the main efforts in public health care should be directed toward eliminating the common causes of sickness and disability: all forms of affliction that cripple persons, personalities, and human relationships. People must learn to accept their responsibility for their own health and that of others. They should appreciate and use their own inner resources and help others to do so. We owe it to ourselves, our families, and the common good to promote health by a healthy life-style of our own.

Other examples could be cited to show that the shape of public opinion decides what will be done in matters of justice, the quality of life, and the pursuit of peace. Almost all the great decisions in the lives of individuals, families, and nations are programmed and somehow predetermined by the quality of current public opinion. This is especially true in an age of democracy.

Those who lack commitment to the formation of good public opinion demonstrate their neglect when they allow or even request those in authority to pass laws and enforce measures which are clearly contradicted by a public-opinion majority. If a government would yield to the pressure of a minority which has failed to make the proper contribution toward forming a consensus public opinion, then the government would be voted out in the next election. Meanwhile it would have had little success with measures that found no genuine echo in the forum of public opinion.

However, we should not forget that legislative actions taken by administrators are also factors influencing public opinion, particularly if the legislators and administrators can give convincing reasons for their decisions. For them, too, the art of dialogue and an intelligent contribution to public opinion are decisive. But all citizens should see in this area abundant opportunities for decisive action.

Freedom of Speech

The right to free public utterance of opinions and convictions, and to active participation in efforts to form public opinion, is a modern acquisition. Nations with right-wing dictators, as well as the Communist bureaucracy, deny and oppose this right. Citizens in such countries have only the right to applaud the measures and ideologies of those in power. Transgressions are severely punished, and anyone who opposes the power cliques is heavily penalized.

But even in healthy democracies the right to free speech has its limits. Freedom of speech is prohibited when the evident intention is the destruction of democracy, especially by violent means, or oppression of the majority or public incitement to crimes against others. As

Christians, we firmly approve freedom of speech within the indicated limits. Our assent presumes two things: first, that we are willing to accept our shared responsibility in the search for healthy public opinion and to acquire the necessary competence for that purpose; and second, that we tirelessly seek truth and justice.

Historically, the public right to freely express and circulate our opinions is founded on the disappearance of arrogant elitism. In the past, secular and ecclesiastical authorities opposed freedom of public expression because of deeply rooted pessimism about the good will and wisdom of the simple people, the "masses," while they themselves exhibited a naïve optimism about their own capacity to know what is right, true, and good. The Roman poet Horace expressed this mentality with the well-known words, *Odi profanum vulgus et arceo* (I detest the common rabble and keep them at a distance). History plainly shows that the hidden reason why powerful minorities excluded the large majorities from the process of searching for truth and from decision-making was simply the group's own self-interest and lust for power.

Even as far back as the last century, Pope Leo XIII (in *Nature of Liberty,* 23) spoke clearly about freedom to offer public opinions and convictions within the Church. "In regard to all matters of opinion which God leaves to man's free discussion, full liberty of thought and of speech is naturally within the right of everyone; for such liberty never leads men to suppress the truth, but often to discover it and make it known." At a later date, Pius XII insisted that the right to participate in the process of forming public opinion belongs to the faithful within the Church as much as within the secular society.

The teaching authorities in the Church have a special obligation to be a learning Church. Listening to the Word of God and proclaiming it cannot be dissociated from listening to people, especially to those of humble condition, of whom Jesus speaks in a joyful prayer: "I thank thee, Father, Lord of heaven and earth, for hiding these things from the learned and wise, and revealing them to the simple. Yes, Father, such was thy choice" (Luke 10:21). To properly understand these words we should remember that in Jesus' time, the religious rulers and the ruling class showed great contempt for the lower social classes, especially for the rural population. Yet most of the prophets came from those parts of the nation.

The Second Vatican Council says explicitly that lay people, too, participate in the prophetic mission of the Church. And it draws this important conclusion: "By reason of the knowledge, competence, or pre-eminence which they have the laity are empowered — indeed sometimes obliged — to manifest their opinion on things which pertain to the good of the Church" (*Constitution on the Church,* 37).

Even in matters of doctrines which allow no contradiction, not only ordained theologians but also lay people can make relevant contributions toward formulating these truths in a way that manifests their fruitfulness for life and makes them more understandable for the various cultures and social classes.

In those questions whose answers are not found in divine revelation, all the People of God are to take an active part in the effort to make proper judgments and find appropriate solutions. The stream of information and competent knowledge — although not that of "competence of office" — flows in from all directions.

On decisions about concrete, historically conditioned problems which require both a knowledge of life and of general principles, no authority has the right to veto the contributions of those who have special competence and valuable experience. For example, we can cite the long debates about taking a moderate interest for capital loans (usury). For centuries, the Church simply reaffirmed the earlier formulations and definitions, while lay people and theologians, although they agreed with the general principles which condemned usury, pointed to the different situation in modern economy. A deeper understanding of the role of interest under the new situation helped also to give more convincing arguments against the sins of usury and exploitation. By not accepting the input from lay people and theologians the Church caused great losses and suffering, and also harmed her credibility in this and other matters.

Our Competence

Our sense of responsibility for searching out and propagating sound opinions goes hand in hand with a sharper awareness of the limits of our competence. If the subject matter concerns vital problems and interests, this does not mean that those who do not have outstanding competence have to be silent. Rather, all should strive to improve their competence. Ordinarily, the art of dialogue is the best method. Through it we learn to distinguish carefully between deeply rooted and matured convictions on the one hand and tentative opinions on the other. Sometimes our best contribution may be a well-formulated question rather than a daring thesis. The formulation and further discussion of the precise questions will induce all participants to more serious reflection, including those who propose the questions.

In the propagation of public opinion, Christians will not think in terms of overcoming the opposition and being declared winners; rather, their purpose will be to simply make their creative contribution in the search for truth and provide authentic solutions to vital problems. Those whose first impulse is to impose their opinions on others will tend to practice manipulation or employ abusive tactics. We recognize them by their clever mixture of praise and blame, reward and punishment; they reveal themselves by their countless deceptive maneuvers. One of their most effective tools is the use of semantics.

Authentic cooperation in searching for and propagating sound public opinions implies dialogue and mutual discussion of values founded on truth and goodness. ''Through loyalty to conscience Christians are joined to other men in the search for truth and for the right solution to so many moral problems which arise both in the life of individuals and from social relationships'' (*Church in the Modern World,* 16).

Only in love and responsibility for the common good, for the well-being of others, and in absolute respect for every sincere conscience can we fulfill our role in this fundamental area. And only by developing our contemplative dimension in the light of God, Father of all, can we avoid the danger of becoming manipulated manipulators.

Prayer

Lord Jesus Christ, you tell us poor sinners that we are "light for the world." Let us never forget that you alone can say, "I am the light of the world." Help us to remember that we receive your light and the mission to be light for others only as a gratuitous gift from you. Teach us to abide by and walk in your light so that we may discern everything in the light of your love and truth.

Lord, we live in an ambiguous world which can easily seduce us unless we have made a firm choice to follow your light, a choice which we must gradually personify with our whole being. Lord, cleanse us, strengthen us, so that we may become more and more transparent; then your light can shine through us. Make us a radiant community of faith, hope, and love, zealous for your saving justice.

Help us to create a "divine milieu" within our world, so that we can work effectively for public opinions which favor justice, forgiveness and peace, truthfulness and sobriety. Strengthen our desire to acquire the kind of motivation and competence that will allow us to exercise a healing influence on civic life through the formulation of good public opinion.

7
SHARE YOUR FAITH

Therefore, take up God's armour; then you will be able to stand your ground when things are at their worst, to complete every task and still to stand. Stand firm, I say. Fasten on the belt of truth; for coat of mail put on integrity; let the shoes on your feet be the gospel of peace, to give you firm footing; and, with all these, take up the great shield of faith, with which you will be able to quench all the flaming arrows of the evil one. Take salvation for helmet; for sword, take that which the Spirit gives you — the words that come from God (Ephesians 6:13-17).

I count everything sheer loss, because all is far outweighed by the gain of knowing Christ Jesus my Lord. . . . and finding myself incorporate in him, with no righteousness of my own, no legal rectitude, but the righteousness which comes from faith in Christ, given by God in response to faith. All I care for is to know Christ, to experience the power of his resurrection, and to share his sufferings, in growing conformity with his death, if only I may finally arrive at the resurrection from the dead (Philippians 3:8-11).

Christians find their identity and discover the radiance of their witness and service by means of faith. In faith they recognize that everything comes from God, the Father of us all. Out of gratitude for the gift of faith and the joy that arises from faith, they dedicate themselves to the service of the Gospel. Experiencing in faith the power of God's grace, they know that the world needs, above all else, a share in this gift.

"God's armor" is not meant for mere self-defense; it symbolizes the faith with which Christians must face the world. This most precious gift gives "firm footing" while bringing "the gospel of peace" to humankind. The "helmet of salvation" is linked with the "sword which the Spirit gives" — "the word of God." This is what the world needs most: God's people sharing the light, joy, and strength of faith with as many people as possible, in gratitude for the gift of faith and joy which the Spirit gives. Saints are marked by the death of Christ and they live in conformity with it; but they are also people who experience "the power of the resurrection."

The *yes* of faith is essentially a grateful assent to the gift of faith; it also indicates our readiness to follow in its path as a community of believers. In reference to our universal call to holiness, the Second Vatican Council speaks to all Christians: "Each one, . . . according to his own gifts and duties must steadfastly advance along the way of a living faith, which arouses hope and works through love" (*Constitution on the Church*, 41).

Meaning of Faith

The real meaning of faith can be perceived from the following example. A parish priest in Rome sent to me an engaged couple. He had refused them a wedding ceremony in the Church because he considered them unbelievers who wanted the ceremony only for the sake of their relatives. They protested that they were believers. The man said, "I believe in Jesus of Nazareth; he was one of the greatest forerunners of Karl Marx and Mao Tse-tung." The woman said, "I do believe in some supreme being." For us, of course, faith is much more than the confusing and arbitrary sentiments stated above. Its content is clear; it covers the whole of God's revelation. We believe in the living God who has revealed himself in Jesus Christ.

Aristotle and other philosophers proved that there must be a prime cause setting all causes in movement. This is true, but it is far from what we believe if no mention is made that the prime cause is a God who is Love.

Deeply touched by the insight that Christian faith is infinitely more wonderful than the insights of the philosophers, Blaise Pascal wrote with his own blood his confession of faith in the God of history: [My God is] " . . . not the god of the philosophers, but the God of Abraham, the God of Isaac, the God of Jacob, the God and Father of our Lord Jesus Christ." Our confession of faith proclaims praise of God arising from our innermost self. It is the life response to the One who is "God-with-us," who calls us to an intimate communion. In faith we entrust ourselves to God, accept wholeheartedly our ineffable vocation, and dedicate ourselves to God's kingdom.

Faith which grants salvation is, for us, a great feast of love and trust. In the Old Testament, God revealed himself as "spouse" of Israel. In Jesus Christ, the Godhead has espoused humanity forever in a permanent covenant between God and humankind. In Jesus Christ, God tells us irrevocably that he enters into communion with us, that his love and mercy is without end, that he calls us to be his holy people, and that he has prepared for us an endless feast in which we share with the Trinity their undying love.

In faith, everyone responds with his or her unique name; but it should be remembered that God wants his revelation and life to be shared by all people. Through our own faith experience — our mission and inner dynamic to share the joy of faith — we give witness to its joyful content as much as possible.

In faith, I rejoice in being loved by him who is Love. But in faith I rejoice equally in knowing that all are loved by God and invited to his love feast. In faith I can marvel, wonder, adore. And what does the world of today need more than this? I cannot imagine a true believer who does not have a strong desire, a yearning, that all people may come to the same joy and strength of faith. So it is natural that Paul, in his eulogy on faith, should invite believers to give themselves "wholly to prayer and entreaty" and to "pray on every occasion in the power of the Spirit . . . always interceding for all God's people" (Ephesians 6:18).

Dimensions of Faith

One dimension of Christian faith is the joyful celebration of the sacraments of faith in the festive community. Faith needs to be shared by singing, praising God in community and, therefore, in all of life. Faith also gives us strength and motivation to bear each others' burdens.

I was deeply saddened on one occasion when I heard a priest boasting that he never had any faith experiences; he could not understand how other priests and lay people could have them. Poor man! There are Christians who have memorized the truths and duties of their faith; but what the world needs most is believers who have encountered faith experiences. It is a great privilege to live with Christians who are on fire, filled with the joy and marvel of their faith. Where such communities exist there is reliable witness to the Gospel and recognition of being sent to share the joy of peace and the Gospel of peace.

The Gospel was and is spread by Christians who are deeply touched by its truths — touched by the unlimited love of God revealed and made tangible in Jesus Christ, and revealed again and again in the lives of saints who direct all our attention to Christ and the Father.

Saints are not interested in the small pleasures of life nor are they constantly concerned about their "self-fulfillment." They bear their own crosses and are willing to accept the burdens of others. Their secret was expressed long ago by the priest Esdras in the Old Testament: "Joy in the LORD is your strength" (Nehemiah 8:10).

Mature Christians look on the moral implications of faith with the same kind of trust that they place in the divine promises. Deeply impressed and changed by his encounter with Saint Francis of Assisi, a Roman cardinal capsulized the life and message of the saint as follows: "We can, we will, we must live the Gospel." The "must" details the plain joy, gratitude, and strength arising by grace from the "we can." This is part of the inner dynamics of love. This is what makes the saints witnesses and their lives a challenge for many people. The saints issue elegant invitations to the feast of faith and to a firm commitment to the kingdom of God.

Faith establishes the conviction that we are invited to be friends of Jesus, children of his Father. Here there is no room for mediocrity. "This is the will of God, that you should be holy" (1 Thessalonians 4:3). Whoever accepts this vocation becomes a blessing for his or her neighbors, for the call implies that "there must be no limit to your goodness, as your heavenly Father's goodness knows no bounds" (Matthew 5:48).

Community of Faith

Christian men and women consider their personal vocation to fullness of life, love, justice, and peace as part of the call of the whole Church to holiness. They know, therefore, that their fidelity concerns all the members of the Mystical Body of Christ, indeed, of all humankind. "If one organ suffers, they all suffer together. If one flourishes, they all rejoice together" (1 Corinthians 12:26).

Our faith is marked by our pilgrim condition. The fundamental option implied in our faith response tends gradually to permeate our whole being, making us ever more conformed with Christ, more detached from whatever might block our pilgrim path, and freer to join God in his liberating love for people. "Then put on the garments that suit God's chosen people, his own, his beloved: compassion, kindness, humility, gentleness, patience. Be forbearing with one another, and forgiving, where any of you has cause for complaint: you must forgive as the Lord forgave you. To crown all, there must be love, to bind all together and complete the whole" (Colossians 3:12-14).

People who, by the strength of their faith, put all this into practice, help humanity to overcome the spiritual "energy crisis" which is infinitely more serious than the physical crisis.

Holy people live neither on an island nor in a ghetto. "All Christians, in the conditions, duties, and circumstances of their life, will sanctify themselves more and more if they receive all things with faith from the hand of the heavenly Father, and cooperate with the divine will, thus showing forth in that temporal service the love with which God has loved the world'' (*Constitution on the Church*, 41).

Prayer

God, our Father, we praise you for the gift of faith which, in so many holy people, has borne fruit in love for the life of the world. We thank you for having revealed in your beloved Son, Jesus Christ, your wonderful design for all your people. We thank you for the community of faith, the Church, for all believers who radiate joy and peace and who help us to understand the real meaning of faith.

I thank you for my parents who enriched me and many of my friends by the strength and abundance of their faith. Through faith they learned to treat us as sharers of the eternal heritage. I thank you for the witness of dying believers who have given me glimpses of what faith obtains and the kind of peace it radiates.

Lord Jesus, you have watched over your mission to proclaim good news to the poor, the downtrodden, the suffering. You have awakened in many sick and depressed people a new hope, and you can truly say to them, ''Your faith has healed you.'' Grant us a radiant faith; and give to the world, which is so impoverished despite all its material success, what it needs most: Christians who dare to be joyful, faithful believers.

8
ASSIST THE ALIENATED

Do not be perturbed, but hold the Lord Christ in reverence in your hearts. Be always ready with your defence whenever you are called to account for the hope that is in you, but make that defence with modesty and respect. Keep your conscience clear, so that when you are abused, those who malign your Christian conduct may be put to shame (1 Peter 3:15-16).

Let us make our approach in sincerity of heart and full assurance of faith, our guilty hearts sprinkled clean, our bodies washed with pure water. Let us be firm and unswerving in the confession of our hope, for the Giver of the promise may be trusted. We ought to see how each of us may best arouse others to love and active goodness, not staying away from our meetings, as some do, but rather encouraging one another, all the more because you see the Day drawing near (Hebrews 10:22-25).

While traveling by train one day, I met a fellow passenger who struck up an intimate conversation with me. His only son, who was to inherit his father's business, had lost the faith. When the father gave him money, the son resented it and immediately passed it on to the poor, arguing that all the father's wealth was the result of an unjust economic system. Yet the son became angry when the father gave funds to pious or charitable works, saying that this, as well as the father's faith, was escapism — the unconscious hypocrisy of a rich man who treats his workers and employees as objects.

We had a long talk, and the man made a soul-searching examination of conscience. It was quite clear that his son's loss of faith was of much greater concern to the father than the future of his business. He was willing to change his conduct radically in the economic and political spheres, with the intent of finally giving his son and others a convincing witness of faith.

I had a similar experience when I lectured in the Philippines on the social implications of the Sermon on the Mount. A very wealthy lady, owner of large sugar plantations, was extremely affected by my words. She realized that her conduct and that of other landlords was causing a deep crisis of faith among the workers, who lived in misery and were totally dependent on their employers. She came to me for advice and help. She was willing to make the most radical changes, giving all who worked for her a just share of the profits and allowing them to participate in decision-making procedures. But she felt threatened by the powerful landlord class which would treat her as a traitor if she would dare to act according to her conscience. What I heard her and some other landlords saying is this: "We must change; otherwise we will be held accountable for the crises of faith and the rebellion of many of our workers!"

Signs of Alienation

One of the most alarming and challenging signs of our times is that almost all of us have some alienated relatives, friends, or neighbors, and we cannot avoid the hard question about whether we might have some accountability for this situation.

The number of "unchurched" people is rapidly growing in many countries of the Western World. Our culture is marked to a considerable extent by a tendency toward unbelief, with little room left for God in the ordering of our social, cultural, and economic world. And a large part of the earth is dominated by a party bureaucracy that uses all its power — from systematic training to secret police, from legislation to methodical manipulation of citizens' minds by the mass media — to inculcate its atheism in the subjugated people.

But this is not the only form of today's atheism. If it were, atheistic Communism would not have much chance to survive because of its bitter fruits. If the rest of the world were composed of authentic believers who bear fruit in love and justice for the life of the world, atheistic Communism would be easily unmasked in its naked misery. One has to be blind not to see the bitter fruits. But the question arises: "To what extent are most of us at least partially blind?"

The Second Vatican Council, with sincere soul-searching, has dealt with the problem of today's atheism (see *Church in the Modern World,* 19-22). And all Christian men and women should meditate on this text as background for a personal examination of conscience.

The Council faces the problem with the same earnestness and from approximately the same angle as the wealthy father of the alienated son with whom we opened this chapter. The Church leaders asked themselves — and each one of us — to what extent we are accountable for the increasing unbelief in the world. The shocking phenomenon of atheism in our own vicinity urges us even to ask ourselves about the "hidden atheist" in our own heart, mind, and conduct. We should, however, avoid extremism in our search for answers. We should not impute to ourselves and the Church institutions such guilt as would seem to leave the atheist guiltless.

Our Response

There are certain wholesome responses we can make. We can renew our interest in the community of faith and thus strengthen and deepen our own faith and the faith of our believing brothers and sisters. Then, in a shared effort, we can more easily rid ourselves of any contamination of atheism and drive it out from the hiding places it has found in our hearts and life-styles. Our main concern, in view of the mission of the Church and the needs of the world, should be to give a convincing witness of our faith and final hope.

The Council's reflections and examinations of the various forms and shades of atheism should open our eyes to the severity of this problem. Its words are a clarion call to a more radical conversion to faith and all its implications in life. For this purpose I want to draw attention to the main problems.

Today's achiever-consumer society offers an educational system mainly geared to attain success as bureaucrats, business and professional people, and scientists, while giving little attention to the formation of mature personalities with depth and breadth of vision and firmness of character.

Young people are rightfully critical of this overemphasis on specialization. The educational system and the whole success-oriented life-style entice both youths and adults to cultivate knowledge for domination, utility, success, and career; and this is done so intensely and exclusively that there is little time to acquire knowledge of wholeness and salvation. Even the behavioral sciences, which customarily make valuable contributions to human growth, frequently deprive themselves of their beneficial dynamics by concentrating on a small sector of research. Thus the spirit of wholeness is lost.

If we are truly concerned about our alienated brothers and sisters, and especially our youth, then we shall do all we can to change for the better our educational system and life-style. If we ourselves, by the grace of God, possess a sense for the mystical and a vision of wholeness, then we shall support all efforts to make this sense and this vision possible in our culture. If we all strive for wholeness and holiness ourselves, then we can have confidence that God will grant in our time many saints who are outstanding in these valuable qualities.

Ernst Bloch, the Marxist philosopher, embodies in his writings one characteristic dimension of the atheist: he cannot and will not believe in a God above us because he refuses to be anybody's debtor. He thinks that it undermines our dignity to thank a God for having granted us unmerited gifts. In view of this, could not our lives and behavior as believers make it more evident that it is this very gratitude and the recognition that everything is a gift of God that awaken our creativity and foster respect and care for others?

There are unbelievers who want to eliminate the God question, or at least subordinate it, in order to honor humankind more effectively as the be-all and end-all of creation. Again, a question: Should not believers show more convincingly that faith reveals the full dignity of every human being, and that nothing can move them more to respect the dignity and liberty of all people than our faith that God has created them in his image and likeness?

The Council alerts us to the fact that there are "unbelievers" who, in reality, do not deny the true God but are protesting against a man-made, false image of God. Could not we believers, through a keener hunger and thirst for a better knowledge of the true God and through adoration "in spirit and truth," help these people to discover explicitly their own yearning for the true God? This asks from us, above all, that we see in Jesus Christ the true image of the Father, who reveals himself in Christ, and that we strongly resist all temptations to make ourselves a self-styled "image of God."

The most dangerous and perhaps the most common form of *Godlessness* (I choose the word consciously) is the absolute lack of interest in the God question, coupled with the same lack of interest in the ultimate meaning of life. Some of today's godless people are not even interested enough to deny God's existence or to think or speak about the subject. Their concerns are totally oriented to success, power, pleasure, and similar objectives.

This form of Godlessness is the strongest challenge for us Christians. We surely cannot alleviate this alienation if the same fleeting and disruptive interests occupy the first place in our own thinking and life-style, even though we also — but in second place — are seeking to know God and serve him. This widespread attitude is, in itself, an expression of polytheism: we place other gods on a par with the true God when we do not reserve for God the first place, indeed, the whole place in our hearts.

The Bible texts at the beginning of this chapter show us that words alone are not convincing and liberating responses to the problems, wounds, and needs of the alienated. Intelligent and competent use of dialogue are important factors here, but prime consideration must be given to total witness by our lives. Then our words and gestures will arise from a joyous, grateful faith and a profound trust in the divine promises.

Faith and life must be harmonized, but never in the direction of the lowest common denominator. If there is a distressing distance between the loftiness of our faith and the quasi-mediocrity of our lives, our alienated brethren should be able àt least to sense how much this pains us and how sincerely we are striving to bridge the gap.

Family Crises

These general reflections on the alienated should be distinguished from the painful experience of good Christian parents when their children go through a crisis of faith and, in some cases, tell their parents that they have lost their faith. This is a very complex affair that differs from case to case; but it is often intensified by atheistic or secularist surroundings in school and aggravated by the mass media and the general environment.

Here is an example of just such a crisis. A certain devout mother and father asked me to accept an appointment with one of their daughters. She came willingly and spoke with true sincerity. She had told her parents that she could no longer receive the sacraments because she had lost her faith. At a certain point in our dialogue I asked her if her search for God was her greatest concern. She answered with a simple ''Yes''; but later she qualified it by saying, ''Maybe my greatest concern is the fear that I shall not be able to give my own children in the future the joyous faith that has marked my parents' life.''

I assured her: ''As I see it, you are by no means an unbeliever. As long as this search takes first place in your heart and mind — despite your present crisis of faith — God will accept it. Perhaps you are now closer to God than you were in your uncritical phase.'' Indeed, she was on the road to a more mature faith. Can all who consider themselves as believers and pious Christians sincerely say that the concern to know God and to do his will take first place in their lives?

Another experience touched my heart deeply. A certain devout family had four boys, one of whom was born blind. All members of the family were always cheerful with the blind boy, but never dared to talk directly about his blindness. For a considerable time everything went well. The boy received First Communion with great fervor, and for two years he received the sacrament each Sunday with his family. But one Sunday he did not join them when they went to Communion. The parents thought it best not to question him. Then one day when it was his turn to say the blessing at the table, he said firmly: "I don't pray anymore; I cannot believe that God is good."

For some years this situation continued. No change seemed to be taking place until one day he began to speak with his parents about his handicap and all its consequences. He explicitly stated his doubt about God's goodness and justice, but his words now sounded like his search was coming to an end. The family began to feel that he had begun gradually to accept his handicap. Then, one Sunday he went with his parents to Communion, giving them an immediate explanation: "I can believe and pray again." And not much later he said: "I think I am now mature enough to receive Confirmation. I know now what it means to be a Christian."

In both of these cases the children were blessed with parents who gave them trusting support as well as abiding love and respect; and they allowed each one time to find his or her way through the crisis. In both cases, also, I could clearly see a growth of faith in the whole family.

The alienated, whether in our own family or in the world that surrounds us, need all the help that we can give them.

Prayer

Gracious Father, I thank you for the gift of faith. It is due to your grace and patience that, despite the gap between my faith and my life, I have remained faithful. And, thanks again to you, I have dialogued with many other believers who have helped my

faith to grow and become more deeply rooted. Praised be your graciousness forever!

Help us all to understand our unbelieving or alienated brothers and sisters. Guide us in our dealings with these people so that we say the right word at the right time, and show us how to accept their challenge by making a firmer decision to live according to our faith, deepening it in all its dimensions.

Holy God, send forth your Spirit. Fill all Christians with the desire to find ways to heal our culture, which becomes for so many a cause of unbelief. Inspire us to form a more lively community of believers and to seek light and strength from the celebration of the sacraments of faith. Help us to take more seriously our mission to be "light for the world."

Father of us all, come to the aid of parents who are at a loss when facing the unhappy crisis of faith in their children. Guide our young people in the dark days of crises so that they may find their way to a mature and firm faith.

9
BE FAITHFUL

Here are words you may trust:
  If we died with him, we shall live with him;
  if we endure, we shall reign with him.
  If we deny him, he will deny us.
  If we are faithless, he keeps faith,
    for he cannot deny himself (2 Timothy 2:11-13).

I am always thanking God for you. I thank him for his grace given to you in Christ Jesus. I thank him for all the enrichment that has come to you in Christ. You possess full knowledge and you can give full expression to it, because in you the evidence for the truth of Christ has found confirmation. There is indeed no single gift you lack, while you wait expectantly for our Lord Jesus Christ to reveal himself. He will keep you firm to the end, without reproach on the Day of our Lord Jesus. It is God himself who called you to share in the life of his Son Jesus Christ our Lord; and God keeps faith (1 Corinthians 1:4-9).

Next to atheism, one of the most alarming signs of our times is the shocking lack of faithfulness. In the realm of marriage, for instance, what kind of example are Christians giving when in the areas of adultery and divorce they break the covenant of marriage in almost the same proportion as unbelievers? A lack of faithfulness is a sign of lack of faith. Where there is unselfish faithfulness and generous forgiveness there is presence of faith. The world needs both the joyous faith and the unbroken faithfulness of these who are in genuine pursuit of holiness.

Holy Scripture sings in sundry melodies the praise of God's faithfulness; but when it praises human fidelity it does so only in view of God's own faithfulness to covenant and promise. We praise God, above all, for his saving justice and mercy by which he restores faithless sinners to renewed constancy. God himself praises the faithful servant and steward in whom he finds a mirror image of his own faithfulness which invites all of us to this stalwart virtue.

Our fundamental option of faith is at the same time a vow of fidelity. If in faith we entrust ourselves totally to God, we will praise him through our constancy. The more firmly we walk on the path of faithfulness, the more our faith comes to its full development.

In the sacraments of faith, the believer consciously meets God's favor and faithfulness. In fruitful celebration we affirm our grateful acceptance of our vocation in allegiance to the covenant by which God binds himself to his people and calls them to mutual fidelity. Our whole Christian life should echo the "Amen" of the liturgy, wherein we solemnly proclaim our "Yes" to him who, by his faithfulness, calls us to abiding fidelity.

God's Faithfulness

Saint Paul explains the deep meaning of the liturgical "Amen" in view of God's enduring trustworthiness. "As God is true, the language in which we address you is not an ambiguous blend of Yes and No. The Son of God, Christ Jesus, proclaimed among you by us . . . was never a blend of Yes and No. With him it was, and is, Yes. He is the Yes pronounced upon God's promises, every one of them. That is why, when we give glory to God, it is through Christ Jesus that we say 'Amen.' And if you and we belong to Christ, guaranteed as his and anointed, it is all God's doing; it is God also who has set his seal upon us, and as a pledge of what is to come has given the Spirit to dwell in our hearts" (2 Corinthians 1:18-22). Whenever we say "Amen" in our prayers, it should be a conscious, trustful confirmation of our fundamental option for faith and fidelity, to the praise of God's own faithfulness.

Jesus is the supreme sign and sacrament of God's faithfulness in his covenant with humanity. In Jesus Christ and by the power of his Spirit he restores us in the covenant and calls us to a renewed and growing fidelity. Christ is the abiding sign of both God's efficacious grace and humanity's response; for, having come from the Father, he has given once and for all his faithful response to the Father in the name of redeemed humanity.

Jesus verifies his faithfulness to the Father's design and covenant by his total readiness for solidarity with us sinful human beings. The One who has taken upon himself the burden of our sins and our misery gives us the gifts of the Spirit so that we can bear each other's burdens. His faithfulness makes his disciples one with each other and light for the world (see John 17:11-21).

Our Personal Fidelity

If we hope to conform ourselves to Christ's faithfulness and become for the world effective signs of his call to fidelity, we have to rid ourselves of wrong ideas about the true meaning of faithfulness. Many people seem to confuse fidelity with habit, with mere passivity. They cling to human traditions which either have lost their original meaning or have never been actual signs of faithfulness to God's holy presence.

Lessons from the prophets and saints encourage us to live the Gospel and faithfully proclaim it ever anew. Conscious of God's nearness to his pilgrim people, we do this even when it means leaving the beaten paths on which many still tread. Saint Francis of Assisi was one of many saints who were first thought to be fools or dangerous innovators.

Faithfulness that arises from a living faith has nothing to do with blind submissiveness or apathetic observance of external laws. Christians who are guided by the Spirit know the ultimate law of faithful love and the deepest meaning of all authentic laws. Their loyalties to causes and groups will always be measured by fidelity to Christ. By faithfully following in his footsteps they can expose any undeserved loyalties.

Our *yes* to God's call to faithfulness implies the courage to take risks, to set out on new paths when necessary — like Abraham, the prophets, the saints, and especially Jesus did in the history of salvation. Faithfulness to the Gospel guarantees Christian identity, but it does so by calling us to a continuing process of conversion and growth, to an ever more creative and generous fidelity.

Our faithfulness to the Church entails much more than mere observance of her laws. For her mission and her inner growth the Church needs Christians who make creative use of their talents and charisms. The faithful servant does not bury his talent in the earth so that it can be given back without risk (see Matthew 25:24-30). What Christian faithfulness means is best expressed by the biblical passage about the gifts and fruits of the Spirit. Fidelity to the Spirit denotes creativity for the life of the world.

Those guided by the Spirit know that true faithfulness to one's own identity and vocation is possible only in faithfulness to God and in solidarity with the children of God. We find our true self in loving service to God and to all humanity.

Fidelity to oneself must be realistic. Even when a devout believer says "I believe," there still may be present a sometimes hidden "I-do-not-yet-wholly-believe." And that means: "I need a further conversion to grasp my faith more fully and to renew my fundamental option to faithfulness." The more I praise God for his faithfulness, the more truthful will be my "I believe."

Our Fidelity to Others

In our response to God's fidelity we can discover the grace-filled possibilities of fidelity to other human beings. Faithfulness to God is the solid foundation of all human constancy. And this, in turn, is an essential expression of our response to God's fidelity to us poor sinners. But among humans, our "Amen" to God has its limits. It is authentic only if we journey together toward an ever more thorough fidelity to God.

The covenant of fidelity between two persons in marriage constitutes a risk, since both partners are sources of risk. And, in a way, the same is true of religious vows where the consecration to God's kingdom implies a covenant between the community and the individual. Yet we can dare this risk without anguish if our mutual *yes* is given and integrated into the covenant with God, the source of all human fidelity. Time and again we are forced to submit ourselves humbly to God's healing and forgiving faithfulness. There we also learn mutual reconciliation and forgiveness as an essential part of covenant fidelity.

Even if a marriage covenant is broken by one of the partners to the point that healing has become impossible — although the other partner has done all in his or her power to save the covenant — the abandoned spouse must strive faithfully to express forgiving love. A refusal to forgive the other's infidelity can destroy the integrity and health of the ''innocent'' one. In the eyes of God, indeed, nobody is ''innocent'' who does not forgive in conformity with God's merciful and healing fidelity.

In Holy Scripture God admonishes us in many ways to be faithful unto death. The divine warnings given to the unfaithful servant are to be understood in the context of God's promises that he wills to perfect the work that he has begun. On God's part, nothing will be lacking if we turn to him in humble and faithful prayer. It is unmistakably the doctrine of the Church that the grace of perseverence unto death is an undeserved gift. But it is equally unmistakable that God wants to give this grace to all the redeemed. We pray sincerely for this gift while constantly striving to honor God's saving faithfulness by forgiving and healing faithfulness toward our fellow human beings. Perhaps not enough has been said and written in today's world about this essential dimension of Christian life.

These efforts and prayers for final perseverance are not evidence of withdrawal into selfish care for our souls alone. On the contrary, the legitimate interest in our own salvation implies total dedication to God's reign and the kingdom of love, justice, and peace. We do not forget for a moment that salvation and holiness imply solidarity; but it would be foolish to imagine that we could possibly help in the salvation, well-being, and faithfulness of the world while neglecting our own salvation and faithfulness to God's gracious love.

Prayer

We praise you, Father! Faithful to your name and with boundless mercy, you have not abandoned sinful humankind in its self-caused misery. In your faithfulness you have gone so far as to send us your only-begotten Son as the faithful sign and witness of your holiness, love, and mercy.

We praise your glory, for in the history of creation and salvation you have chosen us to be not only recipients but also co-workers and witnesses of your faithfulness and mercy, and have not stripped us of this wonderful dignity in spite of our failures.

We thank you, Lord Jesus Christ, that in the work of redemption you have sealed — by your death on the Cross — the Father's and your own faithfulness with the blood of the covenant. We thank you for having offered to the Father, in the name of all humankind whom you came to redeem, your priceless tribute of faithfulness; and we bless you for having called us to join you in praise of the Father by a life renewed in fidelity.

Lord Jesus, send us the Holy Spirit from the Father to teach us how to be open to your kingdom and to be faithful servants and witnesses for the life of the world which is so much in need of fidelity.

10
LISTEN TO AND CARE
FOR THE AGED

Despise no man for being old;
some of us are growing old as well.

Do not ignore the discourse of your elders,
for they themselves learned from their fathers;
they can teach you to understand
and to have an answer ready in time of need
(Ecclesiasticus [Sirach] 8:6,9).

If you have not gathered wisdom in your youth,
how will you find it when you are old?
Sound judgment sits well on grey hairs
and wise advice comes well from older men.
Wisdom is fitting in the aged,
and ripe counsel in men of eminence.
Long experience is the old man's crown,
and his pride is the fear of the Lord
(Ecclesiasticus [Sirach] 25:3-6).

A new branch of science has developed during the last decades: gerontology, or knowledge about aging and the aged, their social role, and their somatic, psychic, and social problems. The way we relate to the aged and their social relevance reveals our fidelity to the past or our lack of it. In the Western World the social problem of the aged is acute, and, in many aspects, it is a symptom of a sick society.

There has always been some kind of generation gap. In the Holy Scriptures we find many words of wisdom about attitudes toward the old, and there evidently was a need to urge the younger generations to honor the aged and to learn from their knowledge. But there is ample evidence also that, generally, the culture of the biblical era showed great reverence and a sense of gratitude toward the aged.

Many Problems

In our times the generation gap has become an acute problem. In a time of rapid cultural change dialogue between the generations takes on tremendous importance, but by the same token it also becomes much more difficult. The cultural diversity between the new and older generation — present even in our vocabulary — has raised barriers to mutual understanding and enrichment. The horizon of understanding has changed profoundly and so has the distance between old and young. The latest statistic of the Federal Republic of Germany, for instance, indicates that only eight percent of the people over sixty-five years of age live in households with children or grandchildren.

Not infrequently, the elderly have the feeling of being ignored. This feeling is particularly strong in nursing homes which are run according to economic considerations alone. In most of the industrialized and urban countries, the suicide rate among the old is very high. Often it is preceded by the painful feeling of a kind of social death, a saddening experience of being considered "useless." In the mass media, and even in government circles, we hear discussions of the "right" of the old and sick to euthanasia. The elderly who feel pushed aside understand this talk as an indirect invitation to disappear from the theater of life. This, of course, is not just a problem for the aged; it is a shocking indication of a sick society.

Two generations ago this was a serious social problem in rural areas when the old did not hand over their farms or business operations to the younger generation at the customary time. Today, men and women retire from their professional activities at age sixty or sixty-five, often when they are still vigorous and not at all ready to become inactive. Many are unprepared for the sudden change and do not know how to profit by their leisure time or how to find an activity that interests them. This is especially true of those who have no meaningful social and cultural contacts, no real friendships.

Add to this the high inflation rate in many countries which robs them of their savings. And even where a high standard of social security prevails, bureaucratic bungling causes distress in some cases. Single women are still widely discriminated against. Women's household work and the education they provide for their children are not considered socially important tasks, and even for paid jobs they do not receive salaries or pensions commensurate with that of men.

While in earlier times senior citizens could be proud of their role and their dignity as elders, the modern cult of youthfulness deprives them of this satisfaction. All this aggravates the task of aging: of accepting the many ailments, the gradual loss of hearing, the diminution of sight and strength.

Some Solutions

Yet the picture is not entirely dark. Much has been done and is being done in many countries to ease the end of life's journey for the elderly. However, the longer life-span and the consequent increased proportion of elderly citizens forces all of us — Church, state, families, trade unions, individuals — to think seriously about the best way to approach the social problems of the aged.

In the Church of the first centuries the aged were community leaders or at least advisors. The term ''elders'' (presbyteri) for priests arose from this situation. It indicates that the older people, the elders, were active in the apostolate. Today in some countries the Church garners many vocations for the permanent diaconate and even for the priesthood from the ranks of the ''retired'' who are still vigorous and willing to use their energies and life's wisdom for the service of God's kingdom in his pilgrim Church.

A considerable number of senior citizens exhibit great interest in continuing education. Church and society should make this and other appropriate privileges and outlets available for them so that their knowledge and life experience may be fruitful for them and for others.

One of the saddest aspects of the aged is loneliness. We should treasure the fact that to visit the sick and the lonely is an important "work of mercy." But this must not be a condescending mercy which might offend the lonely. When we call on the aged we want to let them feel that we enjoy listening to them and learning from them. Children and grandchildren should feel especially privileged to make friendly visits to their parents and grandparents.

The aged, who feel lonely but are still spiritually and physically strong, could best overcome their loneliness by visiting other ailing and lonely people, by offering them some services, reading to them, helping them to pray. It is in this context we understand better the well-known text: "Is one of you ill? He should send for the elders of the congregation to pray over him and anoint him with oil in the name of the Lord" (James 5:14).

"Houses of prayer" in the United States and other countries have contributed valuable inspirational leadership in this area. All the members of these prayer houses participate in spontaneous shared prayer and faith dialogue. But it is especially the older members who dedicate themselves most vigorously to the lonely and sick, bringing them consolation and deeper understanding of their situation.

Many nuns, after successful careers in teaching, have found this apostolate the highlight of their lives. Designated by their bishops to do so, they bring Holy Communion to the lonely and the sick. Some of these aged people, who have been greatly consoled by these visits from nuns and lay people, have written to their bishops asking whether these holy women might not be allowed to administer the Sacrament of the Sick. They gave as reason: "The priest is always in a hurry, rushing in for the anointing and rushing out, while the nuns take time to listen to us and help us grasp the meaning of sickness and suffering." Unfortunately, at the present time the theology of the

Church does not allow this special ministry to people not ordained to the priesthood. Meanwhile, however, senior citizens should continue to visit the lonely and console them with their faith presence and their prayers. And, in a way, that has much to do with the "anointing" of which the Letter of James speaks.

Much more could be done in this area, but for the present this spiritual and pastoral care for the lonely must serve as a stepping-stone for further shared efforts in our struggle to solve the social problems of the aged in our culture.

Prayer

Lord, we thank you for the gift of our older brothers and sisters, for their wisdom, kindness, and their willingness to share their life experiences with us. We thank you especially for those old men and women who radiate holiness and joy. Grant that we — both adults and youths — may gladly follow the guidance which you give through Holy Scripture in our care for the aged.

Assist the old and lonely who are hurt by neglect and social alienation. Help them to resolve their problems and find meaning for their sufferings in the spirit of faith. Enlighten them on how to make creative use of their remaining years, and let them know that their growth in these days will benefit both them and others.

Lord, inspire the influential men and women in state and society to resolve the sometimes shocking problems of the aged and to correct the many injustices under which they suffer today.

Guide your Church so that, following the example of the early Christians, she may be vigilant, wise, and courageous in giving the aged every opportunity to make use of their generous abilities in pursuit of their own special apostolate.

11
GIVE YOUTH A CHANCE

I write to you, fathers, because you know him who is and has been from the beginning.
I write to you, young men, because you have mastered the evil one.

To you, children, I have written because you know the Father.
To you, fathers, I have written because you know him who is and has been from the beginning.

To you, young men, I have written because you are strong; God's word remains in you, and you have mastered the evil one (1 John 2:13-14).

Never be harsh with an elder; appeal to him as if he were your father. Treat the younger men as brothers, the older women as mothers, and the younger as your sisters, in all purity (1 Timothy 5:1-2).

If the aged are an inducement to gratitude and faithfulness to the past, the young are a challenge to hope and a commitment to the future. Of course, all our relationships must be marked by grateful appreciation of the remembered past, but we must at the same time be alert to the present and confident of the future.

Our confidence which looks to the promises of salvation history and our responsibility for the future of ourselves and of humankind will determine our attitude toward youth. The future of our society and our Church will be decided on the amount of our investment in caring for youth, in educating our children and adolescents for co-responsibility. An open-minded dialogue with youth will keep us spiritually young.

In this perspective we can see more clearly the obligations posed by responsible parenthood: the conscientious decision to bring children into the world and to educate them properly. This is a most valuable investment for humanity's future if the transmission of life and life-style are accompanied by cultivation of faith, hope, and love.

Many married couples refuse to transmit life because they have no gratitude for the past, no trust in the future, and no appreciation of the worth of the present moment. Others are simply discouraged by the difficulty of educating children properly in our muddled society. But couples who are blessed by mutual love, filled with gratitude for the gift of life and the hope of life everlasting, and able to make the most creative use of present opportunities will always have the courage to say "Yes" to their parental vocation.

Responsible parenthood in an earlier, more static society achieved an education totally geared to the formation of responsible men and women. In a uniform, harmonious culture, a common faithfulness to inherited traditions and customs served to integrate the children into that culture and its values. Given those conditions, the respect about which Paul writes to Timothy (cited at the beginning of this chapter) was quite possible: parents treating their children like brothers and sisters in Christ, as coheirs of eternal life. In that closed society a "good education" meant also a genuine internalization of faith, hope, and love and of everything that is good, true, and beautiful.

For Christian parents, the goals of education are essentially the same today; but the uniqueness of our present situation necessitates a different emphasis and some additional perspectives.

This new look is a result of rapid cultural change, pluralism of world views and life-styles, and the tremendous influence of the mass media. For many children, TV has become their new foster mother. Mere adaptation to present circumstances — especially if this is coupled with a demand for blind obedience — would simply be a catastrophe. When only passivity and submissiveness are taught in childhood, this usually leads either to rebellion during adolescence and/or to submissiveness to the dominant forces of the environment in which the young adult will live.

Promoting Responsibility

The main emphasis in education, therefore, must be on becoming responsible and discerning persons. The old values are not to be abandoned, but they should be qualified and integrated into a vision of wholeness, holiness, responsibility, and discernment.

Away from their Christian environment, our young people hear much talk about freedom, protest, and the search for self-fulfillment; but they hear little about faithfulness to God, love of neighbor, and self-examination of personal values. It is especially important, therefore, that Christian education should explain and cultivate, by witness and word, freedom in Christ, respect for the freedom and conscience of others, establishment of healthy relationships with God and humankind, creative faithfulness, and discernment which involves healthy self-examination.

Parents, members of the family, teachers, and pastors must be aware that it is normal for youth to go through certain crises — for instance, through a phase of protest and doubt. If they do not profit from this phase, there is little hope that adolescents and young adults will be able to withstand the many dangers of being manipulated by false ideologies or by the mass media which pressures them to accept prevailing immoral fads.

Adults and aging people must continue to learn and relearn how to dialogue with young people, for their reactions change considerably from one year to the next. We have also to free ourselves from a stereotyped idea about youth. There is great diversity among the young, and within every group each adolescent has a right to be seen in his or her own uniqueness.

As young people approach adulthood a certain maturity is demanded of them. They must be prepared to make important decisions about their lives. Foremost among these are a firm determination to be faithful to God and his kingdom and a conscientious effort to choose their life's vocation wisely. Young people should learn from adults that their true identity rests on the strength of their faithfulness. When adults show firmness and consistency in making their own decisions, children will see that the important decisions of life are built on faithfulness to conscience, even in minor matters.

Young Christians should also come to understand that all of life's decisions that are faithful to one's fundamental option are enlightened, strengthened, and enriched by the sacraments. Their baptismal vow is reinforced by their vow of Confirmation, uplifting and sustaining them with the gifts and fruits of the Holy Spirit (see Galatians 5:22). These are the weapons for fighting against humanity's innate selfishness — whether collective or individual or both.

Sharing Responsibility

Participation in church or civic groups and societies should help the young to develop and to exercise their creative energies. Adolescents and young adults should be treated as partners and given the chance to exercise co-responsibility with adults.

Because of the extended number of subjects provided by our educational systems, there is some danger that young people may absorb the subject matter only passively. All those responsible for education in family, school, society, and state should offer the young people sufficient challenge and abundant opportunity for cooperation in creative liberty and fidelity.

This also holds for the political field. A party whose "old guard" insists on clinging to outmoded traditions simply penalizes itself and jeopardizes its future. The experience and wisdom of those who have grown up in dignity and have competently taken their share of responsibility is to be admired; but those who think themselves irreplaceable are lacking in wisdom. When young people have the ability and are willing to acquire competence and able to share in responsibility they should be given the chance to exercise these functions. In all sectors of public life, in society and Church, we need the spirit, courage, and imagination of youth.

Throughout the world the unemployment of youth is a most serious and frightening problem. Not without reason has Pope John Paul II insisted that if this problem is to be dealt with effectively, it must be given high priority. Long-lasting unemployment is not only a grave danger for the psychic and social life of youth but also a great loss for society. It should be evident to all responsible persons that it is easier to create jobs for youth than to rescue them from drug addiction, alcoholism, and violence.

A distinctively Christian vision of hope and solidarity gives us strong motivation to help children and youth to discover and to cultivate the contemplative dimension of life, to find in prayer how to bring genuine harmony into their lives. A good number of today's youth have shown themselves open to faith dialogues, to shared prayer, to joy in the praise of God; however, they should be careful to avoid formalism. They are in search of authentic religious experience. They need holy people to help them along the way.

Prayer

God, our Father, Lord of history, you love children and young people. You rejoice in their growth toward maturity. Give to us older people the openness and joy in creative activities exhibited by the young. Look with favor upon youth for whom today's culture can be a great challenge but also, alas, a great danger.

Give our young people courage to be faithful, to accept their share of responsibility, to search diligently for life's ultimate meaning and purpose, to place their trust in you, and to show a reasonable trust in the future of humanity which depends so much on their active participation in shaping it.

Grant to us adults and senior citizens the ability and the desire to accept youth, to love them as they are, and to appreciate them as persons who can offer dimensions which we are no longer able

to offer. Help us to accept them fully as fellow pilgrims and partners on the road to eternal life and to aid them in their efforts to shape future history to the benefit of coming generations. Inspire us with confidence in our young people, for we can learn much from them.

Lord, grant to your Church the prophetic vision she needs to rid herself of outmoded customs. May she gladly proclaim the Gospel to youth, while living it boldly in today's world. And may she continue to welcome the willing generosity of young people in their efforts to become active workers in God's kingdom.

12
GLORIFY GOD IN YOUR BODY

"Destroy this temple," Jesus replied [to his attackers], "and in three days I will raise it again." They said, "It has taken forty-six years to build this temple. Are you going to raise it again in three days?" But the temple he was speaking of was his body. After his resurrection his disciples recalled what he had said, and they believed the Scripture and the words that Jesus had spoken (John 2:19-22).

Wherever we go we carry death with us in our body, the death that Jesus died, that in this body also life may reveal itself, the life that Jesus lives. For continually, while still alive, we are being surrendered into the hands of death, for Jesus' sake, so that the life of Jesus also may be revealed in this mortal body of ours. Thus death is at work in us, and life in you.

But Scripture says, "I believed, and therefore I spoke out," and we too, in the same spirit of faith, believe and therefore speak out; for we know that he who raised the Lord Jesus to life will with Jesus raise us too, and bring us to his presence, and you with us (2 Corinthians 4:10-14).

The whole human person in all his or her bodily and spiritual reality should be and should continue to become ever more an attractive image of God. A human countenance that radiates joy, peace, kindness, gentleness, cordiality, and compassion is sure to awaken in others a great longing to see God's glorious countenance in

Jesus Christ. The mere sight of hands clasped in friendship, guaranteeing trust and understanding, makes it easier for many to pray to God, "Into thy hands I commit my spirit." We stretch out our hands as a sign of cordial greeting or of reconciliation, and accept gratefully the other's hand as a sign of harmony and fidelity.

Compare this basic human experience with the impoverished image of humankind constructed by that master of manipulation, B. F. Skinner, who sees in human hands only the hands of the ape seizing prey or the hands of controllers and controlled masses applauding dictators.

The human body expresses in basic ways the spirit that lies within. Even at a distance, do we not know from the lift of the runner's head and the speed of his feet that he is a messenger of joy bringing good news? And conversely, when we see the goose step of men trained for war and oppression, do we not also hear in the distance the noise of war and the cry of the oppressed?

Holy Scripture gives us a magnificent vision of the human body. Jesus praises the Father: "Thou hast prepared a body for me. . . . I have come, O God, to do thy will" (Hebrews 10:5,7). His hands dispense blessing, touch the blind, the deaf, the sick, and the lepers with healing love and power. His gracious countenance consoles the afflicted. And, finally, on the Cross he stretches out his arms in all-embracing love for the whole of humanity. His voice not only echoes the cry of the suffering poor but also speaks words of concern, forgiveness, love, consolation, and promise. His pierced heart becomes the fountain of salvation.

Jesus himself calls his body a temple in which God is glorified and which, raised to life again by the Father, will be glorious for all eternity. For Christians, therefore, all temples built by human hands take second place to the bodies of the children of God conformed to the body of the beloved Son, Jesus Christ. Christ has given the greatest sign of love by giving up his body on the Cross for his brothers and sisters (see 1 John 3:16). The love of his disciples, too, must be embodied — revealed in their bodies.

Day by day Jesus offers us the totally embodied sign of his love with the words: "Take and eat; this is my body; this is the cup of my blood, drink from it."

Temples of God

The Christian's body, consecrated in Baptism and sealed by the Spirit in Confirmation, must be honored above all temples on earth; for it is in a unique sense a temple of God, a temple of the Holy Spirit (see 1 Corinthians 3:16-17, 6:19; 2 Corinthians 6:16). Thus the admonition of the apostle, "then honour God in your body" (1 Corinthians 6:20) becomes a theme song of Christian life. Our vocation to holiness, a life spent in giving glory to God, is sculptured into our body. This temple of God, consecrated by God, must be kept holy.

In this same light the Christian concept of chastity must be understood. It excludes any kind of contempt for the body and for the sexual dimension of the human person. The motive for chastity is absolutely positive: reverence for our bodies, for the physical and psychic dimensions of sexuality, reverence for the work of the Creator and Redeemer.

Our prayer as Christians also partakes of this embodiment. We raise our eyes and stretch our arms to heaven as a symbol of turning our hearts and minds to God. We meditate with all our senses, and the whole visible creation invites us to praise God. King David danced before the Ark; it is natural, then, that our African-Christians (and other Christians throughout the world) should express their joy before the Lord, their trust in God, and their surrender to him in sacred dance.

The fundamental truth that the human body, redeemed and consecrated, is a temple presents us with another viewpoint. It is a temple which at all times, in all circumstances and all activities, in joy and suffering, is destined for the glory of God and the building up of the Mystical Body of Christ. The first requirement is that the whole person, in and through the body, radiates purity, reverence, peace, trust, fidelity. We are called to be light to the world and salt to the earth in our embodiment. "The lamp of your body is the eye. When your eyes are sound, you have light for your whole body; but when the eyes are bad, you are in darkness. See to it then that the light you have is not darkness. If you have light for your whole body with no trace of darkness, it will all be as bright as when a lamp flashes its rays upon you" (Luke 11:34-36).

In the light of Christ, men and women in their bodily realities are a kind of sacrament, an effective sign of hope. The appearance of human beings, made in the image of God and able to cultivate and radiate spiritual values with their bodies, is the initial fulfillment of the divine promise and purpose of creation. It points to a still greater promise, the coming of the Word Incarnate, the Word of the Father "made flesh." Having died on the Cross, his glorified body is the supreme promise to the whole of creation and already an awesome fulfillment that opens up a new future. Jesus, crucified and risen, is the supreme, all-encompassing sacrament of hope for humanity and creation.

Members of the Mystical Body

Jesus continues to be a visible sign of hope also in his Mystical Body, the bodily life of his true disciples. They are called to embody this hope through their witness of faith, including their readiness to take upon themselves suffering whenever the victory of love, justice, and peace calls for it.

This witness to hope implies responsibility to the world, an ecological consciousness that perceptibly attests that Christ is the Savior of the whole world. "For the created universe waits with eager expectation for God's sons to be revealed. It was made the victim of frustration, not by its own choice, but because of him who made it so; yet always there was hope, because the universe itself is to be freed from the shackles of mortality and enter upon the liberty and splendour of the children of God. Up to the present, we know, the whole created universe groans in all its parts as if in the pangs of childbirth.

Not only so, but even we, to whom the Spirit is given as firstfruits of the harvest to come, are groaning inwardly while we wait for God to . . . set our whole body free'' (Romans 8:19-23).

It is God's will that we should discipline our body and keep it healthy. His design for salvation is for the whole human being. To abuse our body by unhealthy habits or life-style is to sin also against our psychic health and even against our salvation. By living healthily we reach a harmonious wholeness that affords us greater energies not only for work but also for better human relationships and for the art of radiating peace and joy.

On the other hand, however, our body must never become an idol. This would severely contradict our mission to "glorify God in our body." In our present-day culture, where many people no longer adore God, it is hardly surprising that idolatry of the body flourishes. What Paul warns against under other historical circumstances happens all too easily in a hedonistic consumer society: "There are many whose way of life makes them enemies of the cross of Christ. They are heading for destruction, appetite is their god, and they glory in their shame. Their minds are set on earthly things" (Philippians 3:18-19). Many pamper their body to such an extent that their spirit dissolves — they lose their spiritual strength. Their idolatrous cult of the body causes them to poison it with nicotine, alcohol, and dangerous drugs; they eat too much food while millions of people are dying of starvation.

So often the sports heroes, beauty queens, and movie starlets, who have become idols for their adoring fans, are unconscious of their pathetic show of vanity and their sorry display of spiritual starvation. This is not to condemn healthy sports activities, joyful games and dancing, decent care for the body's appearance, and the admirable art of acting; it is a reminder that the proper scale of values is to be observed in these areas. If we rightly rejoice in the beauty of flowers, why should we not rejoice even more in seeing beautiful men and women whose bodies reveal a beauty tuned into a higher harmony!

Prayer

Lord, our God, how glorious is your name! "What is man that thou shouldst remember him? . . . crowning him with glory and honour" (Psalm 8:4,5). The body of your Son incarnate has glorified you, the Father, and you have revealed in his risen body the fullness of glory and beauty. We thank you for the wonderful composition of our bodies and our calling to honor you in them. We praise you for having revealed that our bodies are meant to be temples, sealed and consecrated by the Holy Spirit.

Grant that we may understand this ever better in its implication for our lives. Pardon us for having paid so little attention to praising your name with respect to our bodies and that of our neighbor.

Lord Jesus, with your body you have given the Father the greatest honor by the very fact that it was dishonored on the Cross, dishonored by sinners.

Enlighten us with your Holy Spirit in times of sickness, suffering, and in the hour of our death, to adore you and the Father in these, your temples. Teach us to enjoy and admire the true beauty of our bodies, as foreshadowing the eternal glory in which they are to shine, and protect us from the danger of making your temples (our bodies) sordid idols.

13
LOVE CHASTELY

Then God said, "Let us make man in our image and likeness to rule the fish in the sea, the birds of heaven, the cattle, all wild animals on earth." . . . So God created man in his own image; in the image of God he created him; male and female he created them. God blessed them and said to them, "Be fruitful and increase, fill the earth and subdue it. . . . "

Then the LORD God formed a man from the dust of the ground and breathed into his nostrils the breath of life. Thus the man became a living creature.

Then the LORD God said, "It is not good for the man to be alone. I will provide a partner for him." . . . And so the LORD God put the man into a trance, and while he slept, he took one of his ribs and closed the flesh over the place. The LORD God then built up the rib, which he had taken out of the man, into a woman. He brought her to the man, and the man said:

"Now this, at last —
bone from my bones,
flesh from my flesh! —
this shall be called woman,
for from man this was taken."

That is why a man leaves his father and mother and is united to his wife, and the two become one flesh.

The man called his wife Eve because she was the mother of all who live (Genesis 1:26-28, 2:7, 2:18,21-24, 3:20).

In the Book of Genesis God manifests his loving design for the world in the words which describe the origin of man and woman. And the Gospel of John enlightens us further about God's word: "The Word, then, was with God at the beginning, and through him all things came to be; no single thing was created without him" (John 1:3).

The whole of creation has somehow the quality of a word, a revelation. But man and woman — because of their mutual rights and privileges — have a special mysterious relationship to God. It was of them that God said, "It is not good for man to be alone." Men and women arrive at truth and self-knowledge when they discover the depth of language in their shared mutuality, in being with and for each other, knowing each other in love. With good reason, researchers think that the origin of human language is the language of love between man and woman, foreshadowed previously in the love songs of the birds and the love calls of other animals.

Marital Chastity

In biblical imagery woman comes into being while the man is in a trance; and she too — like the man — yearns for mutuality and partnership. God himself blesses them when he solemnly speaks, creating them in his own image for communion, companionship in mutual self-giving.

Man and woman should become for each other a truthful "word," an embodied, life-giving word remindful of the divine covenant between them and a loving Creator. Their *yes* to this permanent pact of faithful love and to their vocation of sharing in God's creative love is crowned by the children, provided each helps the other to become ever more visibly an image of God.

There is good biblical basis for today's theological endeavor to treat sexuality as embodied language which, in the marriage covenant and the faithfully fulfilled parental vocation, reaches the summit of communication in mutual self-giving. A basic criterion of marital chastity is the truthfulness of love in their communication. Man and woman "reveal" themselves to each other in their relationships, and especially in the conjugal act if this is in total harmony with their daily-life "togetherness."

Sexuality differs from genitality. *Genitality* refers to the physical, organic expression of sexuality through the act of intercourse and those acts naturally related to it. *Sexuality* is the way of being and relating to the world as a male or female person. It embraces all the dimensions of physical, psychic, and spiritual manifestations experienced by each person. However, sexuality is to be understood neither as the principal identification of the human person nor is it to be considered as a mere addition to it. It achieves its authentic totality only through integration with all our other dimensions and relationships. Its proper use will depend very much on how we recognize and honor the equal dignity and complimentarity of man and woman as gift of God.

The quality of the relationship between spouses — in all circumstances and not just in the expressions of intimacy — will also determine to a great extent the differing overtones in the dialogue between parents and children: father-son, father-daughter, mother-son, mother-daughter. The father, enriched by conjugal love, communicates as father even without explicit words. His child understands this fatherly, masculine language even before he or she can grasp his words. And it is equally true — probably even more so — that a child needs the motherly communication expressed in tender care, constant devotion, intuitive understanding, and cheerful disposition. Happy the child who, in this many-sided dialogue with father and mother, reaps the harvest of a harmonious and rich dialogue between the parents.

Celibate Life

Even celibacy for the kingdom of God is greatly indebted to the multidimensional dialogue between mother and father and parents and children, without which young people would never have reached that level which allows them to love with a Christlike love even those who otherwise are unloved. Consecrated celibacy by no means implies a kind of renunciation of manhood or womanhood. Although those who have freely chosen celibacy for the sake of the Lord renounce genital-sexual satisfaction, all their other means of communication — verbal and nonverbal — are marked by the complementarity and mutuality between man and woman that is part of God's design for humankind.

Of itself, heterosexuality points toward marriage — however, not by necessity but by free choice. According to God's plan, both marriage and celibacy are calls from the Lord to serve in his kingdom. Either call becomes a true vocation when the young person, before God, tries to discover where he or she can best develop his or her capacities to love faithfully and to serve the well-being and salvation of others. Marriage is the ordinary way that this is done, while celibacy, by free choice, is response to a special calling by God to answer the special needs of others. This does not mean, however, that it is something extraordinary for young people to ask themselves whether this might be their true vocation in life. On the contrary, it would be less than normal and a sign of immaturity if a young Christian would never pose this explicit question to himself or herself.

The free choice of celibacy for the kingdom of God can also be a helpful witness for those who remain single because they have not found a suitable mate or because of the breakup of their marriage. This situation can be very difficult in the beginning, but it can become a fulfilled vocation and a road to holiness even as it is for those who chose celibacy in the first place.

Faithful Love

Both the way of marriage and the way of celibacy have their mystic joys and noble opportunities, but both also require a *yes* to the following of Christ crucified and the vigorous renunciation of all forms of selfishness. Only thus can men and women develop their genuine capacity to love as "sexed" persons in their striving for a love far beyond its sexual dimension.

Sexuality, in the sense of bodily union, is fully and truly expressed only in marriage. Only there, consecrated to undying love and fidelity, do the two partners truly become "one flesh." Sexual intercourse outside marriage does bring together, temporarily, two sexual bodies, but it does not make two *persons* "one flesh." However, in marriage, as in other states of life, the attainment of love and fidelity will fluctuate in accord with the commitment of the spouses. For the redeemed, therefore, aiming toward perfection in this area of truthfulness and faithfulness is indispensable in this vocation just as in other areas of moral and religious life.

Next to the choice of state, the choice of mate is one of the important decisions of life. The following criteria should be seriously considered: Am I realistically certain that, if I choose this mate, we will mutually support each other on the path to salvation and holiness? Does this choice arise from a love that comes from God and leads to God? Am I morally certain that this mate and I will be able to keep the covenant of fidelity in good and difficult times until death parts us? Does this choice promise a rich and fruitful dialogue, including intimacy, favorable to our growth in truthfulness and love? Am I reasonably certain that this partner will be a good *parent* of the children we hope to have?

Truthful Love

Truthfulness is a decisive criterion in judging the authenticity of all expressions of love — whether by word, gesture, or bodily intimacy. Hence, in preparing for marriage and in choosing a mate, all words and gestures which awaken false hopes are to be avoided. The path that finally leads to the covenant of faithfulness must be marked by honesty and sincerity.

One of the most relevant consequences of this principle of absolute truthfulness is that sexual intercourse, in the sense of the profound mutual gift and the biblical "knowing each other" — Adam *knew* Eve — is unthinkable outside the marriage covenant. Neither extramarital or premarital intercourse is a truly conjugal experience.

All too frequently a man requests, with passionate vows of love and faithfulness, his girl friend's total bodily surrender. "We consider ourselves as married!" But soon after, having got what he wanted, he declares, "I do love you, but I cannot marry you" — for this or that reason. Time and again I have heard the sad story of these "experiences" which are surrounded by a thousand lying assurances of love forever. Of course, we have to distinguish from these examples the infrequent case of an engaged couple who, only because of external difficulties, are hindered from celebrating their marriage. While we cannot approve their decision to take up a kind of conjugal life without yet being married, we should be fair enough to recognize that here, subjectively, there can be sincerity.

The truthful expression of the mutual dependence of two persons, who are created in the image of God, implies the recognition of the equal dignity of woman and man. Assertions by word or by behavior that woman is inferior to man contradict the truth that both, in their mutuality, are created in the image of God. Or, more specifically, we can say that a man who looks down on woman as inferior does not act according to his dignity as image of God; he is unfaithful to his own dignity and vocation. If equal dignity is fully acknowledged, then the difference between the two contributes to mutual enrichment. Truthful love says in its whole conduct: "It is good that you are; it is good that you are *thus*. . . . " Both man and woman are at their best when they come to a full realization of their high dignity and mutual dependence as image and likeness of God for each other.

How sad it is that in today's world we have to insist that sexuality is not an article for consumption! It is a decided evil that many people are so marked as consumers that this prevalent trait infiltrates even their relationships with the other sex and their own sexuality. Wherever the other is desired as object for the satisfaction of one's own lust, sexuality sinks beneath a shroud of lies and deceptions. Then it becomes cheap, trivial, a source of sadness and disgust. For people who are slaves to senseless consumption in almost every area of life, there is little chance to learn the chaste language of truthful love. But those who uphold their scale of values, while enjoying life and its gifts, are also better prepared to reap a rich harvest of joy in their sexual love and in their capacity to renounce whatever contradicts true love.

In an environment which abhors a rising birthrate, only a truly sincere conjugal and parental love can give convincing witness. Conjugal love is the only abiding source of generous, responsible parenthood. In his encyclical *On the Regulation of Birth,* Paul VI listed the characteristic features of Christian married love as being "fully human, total, faithful, and creative of life."

What our world needs most are holy couples with the beauty and strength of conjugal and parental love, together with Christians who, for the sake of the heavenly kingdom, have renounced marriage and are able to love the unloved who are most in need of them.

Both marriage and celibacy severely challenge today's Christians who live in a superficial and deceitful environment. The manifest integrity of the relationships between man and woman are not possible without the grace of God who is the source of all truth and love; and this has to be acknowledged constantly in humble prayer and thanksgiving. Those spouses who listen to the word of God, cherish it in their hearts and meditate on it together will best be able to accept each other as gifts of God and to travel together on the path to ever more truthfulness, faithfulness, and love.

In all of life, but particularly in the field of chastity, aiming at sheer mediocrity is doomed to failure. On the other hand, those who have solidified their fundamental option to pursue holiness need never be fainthearted. Even if they see that they have a long way to go to reach the ideal, they should not be discouraged. God sees their good will and blesses it.

Prayer

Gracious Father, we extol your design in creating man and woman to your image and likeness. We praise you for redeeming us in all our dimensions. Help us in our state of life to become for each other and for others ever more an image of your love, which is stronger than all the love of fathers and more tender than the love of mothers.

Grant to your Church and to our world holy families. Guide and enlighten our young people in the choice of their state of life. Help them to find their vocation, whether it be marriage or celibacy for your kingdom. Strengthen and console those who, because of circumstances beyond their control, find themselves living celibate lives.

Assist all spouses in the face of crisis, so that they can fully accept each other, pardon each other, bear the burden of each other, and grow in love.

Fill us with your love and truth so that we can live chastely in all our relationships and grow together in the capacity to love the poorest, those unloved and alienated.

14
RESPECT HUMAN LIFE

No one of us lives, and equally no one of us dies, for himself alone. If we live, we live for the Lord; and if we die, we die for the Lord. Whether therefore we live or die, we belong to the Lord. This is why Christ died and came to life again, to establish his lordship over dead and living (Romans 14:7-9).

I have come that men may have life, and may have it in all its fullness. I am the good shepherd; the good shepherd lays down his life for the sheep. The hireling, when he sees the wolf coming, abandons the sheep and runs away, because he is no shepherd and the sheep are not his (John 10:11-12).

For the Christian, divine rather than human life is the highest good for which all other values are to be sacrificed; but to give one's human life in the service of the neighbor is the highest kind of human love (see John 15:13). Thus the tree of Christ's Cross becomes the tree of life. Christ gives his life so that his friends may have fullness of life.

Essential to this fullness of life is the readiness to expose health and life to necessary risks, when it is a matter of serving others, and to do so in the discipleship of Christ. Since life is a precious good from God, this willingness deserves Jesus' praise. That is why he expresses thanks in the morning prayer of his life: "Thou hast prepared a body for me. Whole-offerings and sin-offerings thou didst not delight in. Then I said, 'Here am I: as it is written of me in the scroll, I have come, O God, to do thy will' " (Hebrews 10:5-7).

There are all too many people in the world who want to (and actually do) give legal status to the ''art'' of sacrificing the innocent life of others in order to make their own life more comfortable. They boast about progress in the areas of freedom and right of privacy. These mothers and doctors continue to sacrifice millions of children in the mothers' wombs in order to diminish the guests at the table of life or to prevent the burden of children who might be handicapped.

We can imagine with what wrath German soldiers, who had buried many of their friends, heard propaganda minister Goebbels say: ''The fertile regions of the Don and Kuban are worth the lives of German soldiers!'' Throughout history this has been the way that war ''heroes'' and warmongers have thought and acted. The sacrifice of thousands of civilians in Nagasaki and Hiroshima was excused with the spurious argument that it saved the lives of thousands of American (and other) soldiers. In reality, these were human sacrifices made to the Moloch-ideology which insisted on ''unconditional surrender'' of the enemy, offered so often in past history. Millions of ''undesired'' people were thrown by Hitler into the jaws of Moloch to maintain the myth of a superior race, just as other millions were sacrificed by Stalin to give homage to his cult of dialectic materialism. And the most horrifying aspect is that these men easily found willing collaborators.

These events of ancient and modern history should disturb the conscience of all decent people. They should be asking themselves what to do in order to prevent similar sacrifices to the devouring false gods of the future. A Christian who believes in the Good Shepherd, and accepts his supreme commandment of love of God and neighbor as rule of life, must face these questions explicitly and make every effort to acquire the necessary competence to engage in this continuing battle for worldwide respect for human life.

Not only our own but also our neighbor's lives, indeed the lives of all people, are entrusted to our shared responsibility. In a world where people's needs cry out to us from every side and where we can exercise worldwide influence, we would be following the bad example of the priest and Levite in the biblical parable if we did not care for the life and health of other people. By imitating the unselfish actions of the merciful Samaritan we can rescue many who have fallen into the hands of "robbers."

Supporting Life

Here is an example of what people can do. If Christians would spend as much for the healing of lepers as they spend for harmful tobacco and alcohol, the plague of leprosy — which at the present time has about thirty million people in its grip — could be quickly overcome. Is this too much to ask from people who believe in their vocation to holiness? Even those who are not slaves to any harmful addiction should, in thanksgiving, spend generously for others who so need their help.

I stand before each of my readers as a beggar for lepers. In many parts of the world I have seen their sufferings. Every diocese, or at least every country, has (or should have) a collecting agency to provide help for the healing of lepers and the prevention of leprosy. But the funds must flow more generously to these merciful endeavors.

Hundreds of millions of people suffer starvation, and millions of lives are threatened each year by hunger. These persons stretch out their arms to us for urgent help, indeed for generous help.

Our crusades against planned abortion, against war and mass starvation all must go hand in hand; otherwise we would not be consistent and credible. Those protesting loudly against the threat of nuclear weapons, which can destroy the whole of humankind, do well. But all, while protesting against these striking evils, should ask themselves if they are also willing to make their personal contributions to alleviate dangerous hunger and contagious diseases or to take political action to bring about more generous help to the poorest countries. And, further, they should ask themselves whether they are caring properly for their own health or endangering the health of others. (I refer, for example, to the guilt feelings of many lung and throat cancer patients who formerly were heavy smokers and to the conviction of many doctors that smokers polluting the air are sometimes the cause of such damage to others.)

Generous land developers and able medical missionaries are the merciful Samaritans of today. During the course of a visit to a poor area of Africa I met two Italian ladies — medical doctors — assisting there. I was told that originally they had volunteered for only a few years; but, seeing the tremendous misery and need, they continued to prolong their stay — even with the realization that this meant nothing less than giving up their chances for marriage. They have saved many lives. We could do something similar without such a high price just by making generous offerings for the needs of others, offerings which in many cases can be lifesaving.

Saving Life

Capital punishment is a "life" subject. There were and still are two opposing opinions in the Church. Some persons — chiefly the fundamentalists — justify the death penalty by quotations from the Old Testament. Others oppose it by insisting on the revelation of God's mercy in the New Testament and by pointing to the basic truth that Christ died on the Cross for us sinners who might have deserved eternal punishment.

Since my earliest writings as a moral theologian I have opposed, on principle, the death penalty. I am convinced, at least in principle, that this conviction is more in keeping with the compassionate love of Christ and the heavenly Father for sinners. But besides that, there are historical reasons. I allude especially to the German State under Hitler, one of the greatest of mass murderers. Although modern judges are not to be accused of such crimes against life, they would do well to remember what happened in Hitler's time and, humbly, to forbear passing the death penalty on people found guilty by fallible human judgment.

Although the above reasons are not so telling in other countries, it cannot be denied that even in such democratic countries as the U.S.A.

minorities often receive the death penalty for certain crimes while the privileged class receives disproportionate or no punishment at all for the same kind of crimes. In general, we can assert that there exists such a shameful human tradition of judicial murder by communities all over the world that it is best to break away totally from this way of acting and to concentrate instead on preventive measures and rehabilitation.

However, this is an area where different opinions have existed and still exist within the Church, and we should be tolerant of others who think differently. But one thing must be vigorously asserted: A state which refuses to protect the innocent life of the unborn can claim no legitimacy for passing death penalties, since the only good reason for the death penalty is protection of innocent life against violence.

Prayer

O God, Creator of all life, you seek not the death of the sinner but his conversion so that he may live fully. We all live by your generosity and mercy. We thank you for the wonderful gift of being, to which you have added the promise of eternal sharing in your life and bliss. You have called all people to eternal life. Help us through your grace to assist each other on our road to fullness of being and eternal life.

We praise you, Father, for having sent us the Good Shepherd who has laid down his life and thus has favored us with the sublime opportunity to love our neighbors in the service of life, justice, and peace. Make us witnesses to our faith and hope in the resurrection of the body.

Merciful God, since earliest times men like Cain have murdered their brothers and sisters in time of peace and even more in time of war, thus horribly dishonoring your name as Father of all. We grieve especially because so often even Christians who call you "Father" have neglected and even defied your mandate to serve and save life, thus sinning at least through inactivity or

complicity. Before you judge us, we all must humbly ask ourselves if we have shown gratitude for the gift of life by a wise and generous shared responsibility for the life and health of our fellow human beings.

Forgive us, Father, for having damaged our own lives and those of others by an unreasonable, unhealthy life-style. Make us signs of healing goodness and peace, angels of nonviolent commitment to peace and justice.

15
HEAL YOURSELF AND OTHERS

John too was informed of all this by his disciples. Summoning two of their number he sent them to the Lord with this message: "Are you the one who is to come, or are we to expect some other?" . . . There and then he cured many sufferers from diseases, plagues and evil spirits; and on many blind people he bestowed sight. Then he gave them his answer: "Go" he said "and tell John what you have seen and heard: how the blind recover their sight, the lame walk, the lepers are made clean, the deaf hear, the dead are raised to life, the poor are hearing the good news — and happy is the man who does not find me a stumbling-block" (Luke 7:18,19,21-23).

Holy Scripture leaves no doubt that healing the sick is an essential dimension of Christ's mission. On some occasions it seems that, for him, healing is more urgent than preaching the Good News. Or rather, healing the sick is a privileged form of proclaiming the Good News of the Messianic time. He heals even on the Sabbath, although he knows that this makes him a stumbling block for the legalists.

The Sermon on the Mount is introduced by this remark: "Everyone in the crowd was trying to touch him, because power went out from him and cured them all" (Luke 6:19). Healing is a manifestation not only of his power but, above all, of his compassionate love. Jesus seems to see in disease an aspect of the powers of evil, a sign of a world in need of redemption and liberation. Healing the sick is also a symbol of the healing of those with broken hearts. Yet, Jesus vigorously rejects the prevailing opinion of his time which deemed the sick and/or their parents as cursed because of their sins (see John 9:22).

Especially lepers had to suffer severely from this notion. They were outcasts, untouchable and despised as the most miserable of sinners. Jesus reached out to them, healed them, and reintegrated them into society, thus restoring them to religious and civic esteem.

By his healing activities Jesus glorifies the Father. But he also points out that patient suffering is one way of following him on the way of the cross. Nevertheless, acceptance of suffering and illness in ourselves and others has a positive meaning only if we do everything possible to heal whatever can be healed.

Modern medicine has won many battles against disease and will win many more. Yet, at the same time, the modern world, with its unhealthy life-style and its reckless abuse and destruction of the environment, has opened the door for legions of evils. This warns us that we should not simply resign ourselves to sickness as if it were sent by God; we should not blame God for the many evils which we have brought upon ourselves.

Nevertheless, while doing our best to heal what can be healed and removing the causes of sickness where they can be removed, we can resolutely accept the burden of shared responsibility for what cannot be healed — even as Jesus took upon his shoulders the Cross which human iniquity had prepared for him. At one and the same time we may detest all sins, including those which have disrupted our world and caused diseases, while we bear our own crosses in time of illness. We would not be true disciples of Christ if we cursed our sufferings. And obviously, our just rebellion against the sinful causes of evil must never become rebellion against God who, in time of sickness, gives us strength to endure every ordeal.

Health of Body and Soul

Before we consider the important question of what health has to do with salvation and holiness, we should clarify what we mean by human health.

Health does not consist of the mere bodily capability of working, although this is an excellent quality to have. Nor is it sheer bodily strength, especially when the higher faculties that reach out for truth and search for ultimate meaning are neglected.

Human health can be defined as the highest possible embodiment of the spirit and the noblest spiritualization of the bodily dimension. One person's body may have a surplus of physical vitality but a pitiful lack of openness to the spirit and to healthy human relations. Another person's body, although physically suffering, may be completely open to the spirit of goodness, joy, peace, compassion, and serenity. A well-trained body makes for an excellent person if it is guided by its higher values.

The physical integrity of the body and all its vital parts is a precious good entrusted to our personal and shared responsibility. But this kind of integrity falls short of human wholeness and health. On the one hand, there are ways of risking health which do violence to wholeness and our vocation to wholeness. On the other hand, there can be generous commitments involving substantial risk to physical health which are genuine expressions of the pursuit of holiness in the service of neighbor and the common good.

Of great relevance to wholeness, salvation, and promotion of salvation is *psychic* health. But even here we have to be cautious in our evaluation. Just recently I was informed of the death of a dear friend, a genial man in many respects. After undergoing the shocking experiences of Hitler's war, his proneness to depression caused a nervous breakdown. Of a sudden, he began to speak out publicly against the war crimes of Hitler; only the psychiatrist could save him from being executed. Later we often talked about his situation which he could shrewdly analyze. Thanks to modern medicine, his condition could be kept under control; but what helped him more than the drugs was his astonishingly serene conformity with God's will. Beyond and above the psychic illness there was a feeling and force of wholeness which allowed him to accept and transcend his handicap.

Psychosomatic medicine, psychoanalysis, and the various schools of psychotherapy have revolutionized the concepts of health, sickness, and healing. Attention centers largely on the phenomenon of neuroses. In a neurotic state, essential energies are blocked by unfavorable conditions in the environment, by disturbed human relationships, and by unresolved personal problems. These forces, even though they are not properly brought to the fore or cultivated, are not dead. When they do not find a healthy outlet they turn inward, causing extreme tensions and singular reactions. However, it would be a great error and an injustice to malign persons suffering neuroses or to impose moral condemnations on them. A neurosis should be understood as a cry from the depths for inner wholeness and healthy relationships, a cry for someone who can help to uncover these inner forces and their meaningful use.

Health and Wholeness

Victor Frankl, the father of logotherapy, has drawn our attention to *noogenic* neurosis which develops in an existential vacuum when the inborn desire for ultimate meaning is frustrated. The conscious and frequently unconscious loss of meaning or the repression of the search for meaning disturbs both somatic and psychic health. The lack of harmony between achievement or pleasure-seeking and failure to establish a scale of values affect the person in all his or her dimensions and relationships. Healing requires a new impetus in the search for meaning and the gradual realization of the level of meaning which insight provides. Here we see the fixed relation between health and wholeness-holiness.

The experiences of logotherapists suggests that those who graciously and patiently help other persons in their search for meaning provide the kind of therapy that is so necessary in seeking redemption. Persons who are physically or psychically sick or handicapped are most seriously threatened in their wholeness and salvation if they fail to search for the meaning of life or refuse to find an acceptable meaning for their suffering. To feel secure in the attainment of a value which fills the heart and mind is a giant step on the road to human health.

There are two extreme positions here. Thomas à Kempis, in his

Imitation of Christ, thinks that nobody becomes holier through illness, while Saint Hildegard says that "God's dwelling place is normally not in a healthy body." Both expressions have to be evaluated in their context. We should not wait until we are sick before striving for holiness; and we should not doubt that, with God's help, illness or any kind of suffering can provide opportunities to achieve holiness. Saint Hildegard insists with Saint Paul: "Power comes to its full strength in weakness" (2 Corinthians 12:9). But she also rightly warns that we should not weaken our health by imprudent asceticism or an unhealthy life-style. God does not promise special help if we imprudently and irresponsibly jeopardize our physical or psychic wholeness.

In the tedious struggle against sin and the constant striving for holiness, an especially profound experience of God's purifying fire can deeply affect a person in need of thoroughgoing purification. But it is equally true that a sincere fellowship with Christ and the experience of God's nearness and love create astonishing energies for building wholeness and human health in all its dimensions. The inner peace and lasting serenity, which are God's gifts to those who seek only to conform with his will, provide amazing strength to cope with life's tasks and tests. This inner harmony, reflecting union with God, is also a blessing for bodily and psychic health.

Viktor von Weizsäcker, a prominent physician, tells us that "illness is a mode of being human." We have to pass through the experience of weakness, unhealthiness, and death on our way to eternal life. If — in the various situations of life — we accept God's design to the best of our ability, then even grave suffering and illness can become times of grace. Illness reminds us of the finiteness and frailty of earthly life; it challenges us not to lose sight of heavenly life with God. Thus it is an offer and an opportunity for deeper reflection and clearer direction toward our abiding vocation. We have to see both risk and opportunity in illness. In the school of the crucified, illness presents us with a favorable time to become better friends of Christ.

Prayer

Protect us, O Lord, from all sinful neglect of our health. Heal us, for we have sinned against you and against our own wholeness. Grant that a healthy soul may dwell in our body and radiate purity and peace, whether our body be weak or strong.

Grant us a deeper insight into the meaning of life, health, and unhealthiness. But, above all, bestow on us that love which guarantees that everything — suffering and ill-health included — will redound for our good.

Give us insight, grace, and strength to care more for salvation and holiness than for mere physical health, and yet to care enough for health not to lessen our striving for holiness and unselfish service.

Gracious God, assist and console the sick. Enlighten and heal those unfortunate persons who have failed to search diligently for the true meaning of life and, as a consequence, are sick in body and soul. Send them loving and competent people to guide them in a renewed yearning for a meaningful life.

16
MEDITATE ON YOUR MORTALITY

*But the truth is, Christ was raised to life. . . . In Christ all will
be brought to life; but each in his own proper place: Christ the
firstfruits, and afterwards, at his coming, those who belong to
Christ. Then comes the end, when he delivers up the kingdom to
God the Father, after abolishing every kind of domination, authority,
and power. For he is destined to reign until God has put all enemies
under his feet; and the last enemy to be abolished is death.*

*When our mortality has been clothed with immortality, then the
saying of Scripture will come true: "Death is swallowed up; victory
is won!" "O Death, where is your victory? O Death, where is your
sting?" The sting of death is sin, and sin gains its power from the
law; but, God be praised, he gives us the victory through our Lord
Jesus Christ (1 Corinthians 15:20,22-26,54-57).*

*For, as I passionately hope, I shall have no cause to be ashamed,
but shall speak so boldly that now as always the greatness of Christ
will shine out clearly in my person, whether through my life or
through my death. For to me life is Christ, and death gain; but what
if my living on in the body may serve some good purpose? Which
then am I to choose? I cannot tell. I am torn two ways: what I
should like is to depart and be with Christ; that is better by far; but
for your sake there is greater need for me to stay on in the body
(Philippians 1:20-24).*

Death is surely our abiding companion. Our lives are passageways to death, whether we like it or not. It is better to like it; then it will be easier for us to take it fully into account.

Christians who consciously live by faith are different from unbelievers. They are familiar with Brother Death. They know its awesomeness; but they rely on God's firm promise that, with the help of his grace, their faithful confirmation of their vocation to holiness will make the day of their death a harvest feast, a victory celebration of their fidelity to Christ, a coming home to the Father.

Those who banish the thought of death are doomed to an unreal mode of existence. With no convictions about life's final truth, they are swayed by the masses who do not want to know where they are going. And those who plan their lives as if death did not await them are more "under the law of death" than they suspect. This "death repressing" attitude, dwelling and rebelling in the subconscious and unconscious mind of persons who attempt this desperate evasion, will play its sinister and damaging role in all that they do. A stubborn determination not to face death and not to accept it as part of a person's truth blocks all access to life's truth.

In the apostle's Letter to the Philippians we see how our *yes* to life, with full acceptance of the fact of death, gives us maximum freedom to live life authentically. Christ himself becomes our life and our joy. For us, Paul's two sayings, "death is gain" and "to me life is Christ," are inseparable, just as Christ's death and Resurrection are inseparable. For believers, acceptance of death will open up to them a life in Christ Jesus.

Whoever affirms life's and death's final meaning as consciously and trustingly as Paul did will experience the same liberation from slavish fear of death and law. A dying man I know expressed this beautifully when his doctor was nervously searching for words to tell him that death was near: "Doctor, are you having trouble telling me that I am going to die? Why? All my life I have lived for this day!"

How different are the words of those who are under the "law of sin and death," of sin-solidarity and flight from God! Look at the evasion practiced by the family whose members unanimously agree to deceive their dying father about the seriousness of his situation — all in slavish obedience to a doctor who prefers this kind of "practice." The priest is called in only after death to perform a "ceremony" for the sake of public appearance.

Solidarity in Christ (complete union with him through his redemption) leads to the joyous song of praise: "God be praised, he gives us victory through our Lord Jesus Christ" (1 Corinthians 15:57). The same song of victory resounds also in the Letter to the Romans: "In Christ Jesus the life-giving law of the Spirit has set you free from the law of sin and death" (Romans 8:2).

This victory of salvation-solidarity happens time and again in devout families. John, who always thanked God for his "holy wife," could not stop his tears when he saw that she was dying. He appealed to the Lord: "Did I not always pray to you to let me die before Francisca? What am I without her?" The Lord's response came through the lips of his dying spouse: "But, John, how can you complain? Isn't it the Lord's right to decide about the hour of our death?" John stopped weeping then; and from that time on he continued to thank God for the gift of his wife who, for so many years, had exemplified holiness — even to the very moment of her death. And at the time of his own death, he faithfully put into practice the lesson she had taught him. When he told his eldest son that his own death was near, the son reminded him that the rest of the family, who were on their way, would be gathered there in a few hours. The dying father said: "The Lord is calling me now; I cannot wait. Give them my greetings; bid them good-bye for me."

Could John and Francisca leave their children and friends a greater heritage than this witness of their faith and saving-solidarity?

Our Attitude

A right attitude to illness and death is not only an extremely important personal matter; it is also a basic question of social ethics.

The world needs our effort, our witness and wisdom for the liberating truth.

Ivan Illich rightly sees in this *yes* to frailty, illness, and mortality the foundation of an authentic human health and healthy relationships. It is a matter of shared courage to accept all of life's dimensions in the fullness of their truth. Not only the life of individuals but also the profile of society itself is transformed when we frankly acknowledge that we all walk together in the shadow of death.

This freedom to accept each day of our lives as an approach to death, and to sense fully this limited earthly life, is anchored in our faith in the Resurrection of Christ and in the divine promise of our own resurrection. If Christ is truly our life, then the experience of the loving nearness of God and the intimate communion of life with Christ assures us that this community of love cannot end with our death but is designed by God for all eternity.

What a blessing it would be if the lives, actions, and words of all men and women in the healing professions were inspired by these basic attitudes!

In a certain sense, death, our mortality, is natural. Our whole biological frame is directed toward growth and gradual decrease, leading naturally one day to death. However, *our* dying is something totally different from that of plants and animals. Our death is a decision to be consciously faced.

Yet, there is something very unnatural about human death — especially the death of sinners. The flood of sin, growing from its poisoned beginnings into a stream of anguish and terror, is not willed by God. Sinners, closing their hearts to redemption, making their choices against salvation-solidarity and thereby locking themselves into the guilt of sin-solidarity, cannot blame God or nature for the anguish and futility surrounding their deaths. We can say simply, with Holy Scripture, that their deaths entered into history through sin.

Given the unnaturalness of unredeemed sinfulness, it is "natural" for the sinner to banish the thought of death, to rebel against it, and to suffer the terrible consequences of this flight and rebellion. But the redeemed who, by God's grace, build their lives on faith in redemption and resurrection, are indeed liberated from the "law of death" which the sinner chooses. At death — by the power of grace and faith — a real transformation takes place: the believing redeemed who die with Christ take on an abiding "life in Christ."

Here, then, we should call to mind the tension between the "already" and the "not-yet." In accord with God's design we are all meant to be liberated from the terrible death which befits the sinner, as sinner: a death which is a sign of solidarity in sin and futility. Christ, accepting the anguish of the most painful and humiliating death on the Cross, echoing the anguished cry of sinful humanity, "My God, my God, why hast thou forsaken me?" has offered himself as redemptive sacrifice in the supreme act of saving-solidarity. He who, by divine mission, is saving-justice and saving-solidarity, he who is without sin, has consented to the Passover through the Red Sea of sin-solidarity and its bitter consequences.

We, who put our faith in Christ's saving death and Resurrection, are liberated from death as punishment and final despair. Yet death still possesses some painful dimensions even for true believers. The first is that most of us are not yet fully detached from all sin, and we are not living fully in Christ. Physical pain and mental anguish brought on by separation from loved ones — which, in accord with God's design, is a sharing of saving-solidarity with our Redeemer — give us abundant opportunities to overcome, with God's grace, this laxness in our faith. But a more important and consoling fact is that, for those who are called to share Christ's redeeming action in the world, it is — in a way — "natural" that they consciously accept the pains of illness and death "for the life of the world." It becomes the solidaric passover from death to life, from the inglorious death of the unredeemed to the glorious death of the redeemed; it is the seed that falls to the ground to become new and wonderful life.

We firmly believe this important truth: for the believer, as such, death is in no way a curse or punishment. Even the painful fact of knowing that we need further purification is pervaded by the consoling light of the Paschal Mystery. The final transformation at death is most apparent in those who accept death, with all its external circumstances, as a gracious presence of the Giver of eternal life who brings to completion whatever he has begun and favored throughout our lifetime.

One of the most precious faith experiences we can have is to be present at the bedside of a dying Christian who gives convincing testimony that "Christ is my life and death is gain." For ourselves and those we love, indeed for all believers, we should never stop praying for the undeserved grace of perseverence in God's love. It is also a matter of fundamental saving-solidarity that we help the dying to receive the consolation of the sacraments of faith as frequently as possible and see to it that they receive all the pastoral care they need.

Our Responsibility

Since the kind of death we are to die depends essentially on our fundamental option for either solidarity of salvation or solidarity of evil, we also have to face our co-responsibility for other people's "unnatural" death and our own risk of unnatural death in any of its various forms and meanings. As active Christians we shall do our best to ensure that no one within our sphere of influence will die the fearful death of the unredeemed, a death encountered in guilt and alienation, a death endured after desertion or open rebellion. The world needs this commitment as much as it needs our involvement in the crusade for healthier social structures.

Also under the heading of "unnatural" we consider here, first and foremost, death by suicide or murder. We all have to ask ourselves how many other people have participated actively or passively in the process of decay that leads to such outbreaks of unnaturalness.

Penal law speaks of "manslaughter" when punishable negligence contributes to the unnatural death of others. But it would be a grave error to heed only the definitions and limits of penal law. Negligence can take a thousand forms. Reckless driving is one of the most frequent, but the more than one hundred thousand deaths on the earth's highways each year cannot all be blamed on reckless driving. The fault may also lie with irresponsible drivers who take "just one more" drink before driving, with careless drivers who neglect the maintenance and repair of their cars, with those who drive in periods of depression, anger, and near-exhaustion, and with countless others who are guilty of culpable negligence on the road.

Millions of people burn out life's energies and shorten their life-spans by immoderate use of alcohol, drugs, and tobacco. Their sometimes early deaths — "unnatural" in our sense of the word — point to the frightening evil of collective sin: neglect by parents and educators, by pastors and moral theologians, and by doctors who dare not alert people about their senseless life-styles because they do not want to be accused of "moralism" — while, indeed, their own neglect in this matter is immoral.

It would also be immoral to assume a judgmental attitude that places all the blame on those who, for various reasons, die early or violently. Redemption does not allow us simply to point to culprits. Rather, we should look after our own responsibility and continue to examine our own consciences.

It seems strange that people today — even many doctors — accept rather easily the taking of early life in a mother's womb and the foreshortening of the life-span by abuse and unhealthy life-styles, while, at the same time, they spare no effort to prolong the irrevocable death process in adults by highly sophisticated and expensive means which benefit neither the unconscious patients nor their families.

This phenomenon is at least partially the result of the "death repressing" attitude described at the beginning of this chapter. The enormous cost-consuming efforts wasted on artificial and useless prolongation of the death process could be better used to rehabilitate the handicapped and to assist families with handicapped children.

Euthanasia

While liberation from "the law of death" categorically excludes suicide and irresponsible shortening of one's life-span, it enables us to look serenely toward natural death in conformity with God's will. In this context we have to combat the modern attitude toward euthanasia. If we Christians are to form a healthy public opinion in this area, this is one of the debates in which we must participate with special competence.

Etymologically, *euthanasia* means "dying well." Understood in a Christian sense, this includes: a striving for a good life, which is the best preparation for a good death; a heartfelt assent to life and death; a loving care for the dying, given by their families, friends, and neighbors, and especially by the members of the healing professions; an attempt to alleviate the sufferings of terminal illness; and a reassuring effort to emphasize the consolation of faith.

An important service which the Church owes its sick members is to console and strengthen them with the sacraments while they are still able to receive them in full consciousness. The Anointing of the Sick should never be deferred until the last moments. It is not only a sacrament for the dying but also for the sick, that they may profit from the time of illness and eventually recover.

In today's medical-ethical discussions, euthanasia means: (a) the refusal of helpful measures in order to speed the arrival of death; (b) the use of measures intended to cause death directly.

Theologians, backed by the teaching authority of the Church, categorically condemn both of the above methods. Euthanasia is an attack on God's sovereignty over death and life. Consciously to cause one's own death (or to ask others to cooperate in it) or to refuse helpful means to which the dying or gravely ill person has a right — these are all arbitrary acts deserving condemnation. If death-promoting methods are used without consent of the sick person and with the explicit intention to cause death, this is, of course, simply murder. Only under the barbarous regime of Hitler was this merciless "mercy-killing" called "euthanasia."

Euthanasia, in the sense of refusal of helpful treatment with the purpose of shortening life or in the sense of direct measures to accelerate death is not only a moral problem but also, in our times, a legislative problem. We do not mandate the state to place penal sanctions on all transgressions of ethical principles; but to legalize euthanasia, or to legally declare that the state leaves such decisions to private individuals, is a betrayal of the state's specific duty. Its duty is to protect the weak and the aged, the sick and the handicapped, to protect the sacredness of human life.

It is easy to predict the effects of legalized euthanasia. Those who feel that they have become burdens to their own little community or to the state would be in constant fear: "Will it be today or tomorrow that the state will choose for me to disappear from the theater of life?" Then, too, our basic trust in doctors would be undermined if the medical profession would agree with such legislation and show willingness to kill ailing people on request. The argument that legislation is proposed only for those who freely request it is not valid. With the legalization of euthanasia many people would begin to feel unjust pressures and would be subjected to downright manipulation.

Quite different is the use of intense pain-killers or the courageous attempt to save life by unusual means when ordinary means have failed, even at the risk of shortening life unintentionally. These do not conform to the concept of euthanasia which we radically reject.

Right to Be Informed

Another matter which concerns each of us personally, and is highly relevant for Christians who participate in the formation of public opinion, is the right of patients — especially the terminally ill — to be truthfully informed about their situation. Truthfulness is essential for healthy personal relationships and for healthy communities. It has special relevance in the patient-doctor relationship.

Of course, an unfavorable diagnosis is not a truth that can always be communicated bluntly and instantly to the sick person. Failure to give all the facts at once is not at all a lie if the intention is to tell the truth step-by-step in the best possible manner. Doctors, nurses, and members of the family can tactfully probe to what extent the patient is ready to hear the full truth or to receive further information. It is best for the patient to help the doctor by showing his or her readiness and courage to face the truth. When it was a question of reappearance of my larynx-cancer I told the doctor emphatically that I support the principle, "Only truth can liberate us." I saw how the doctor immediately felt at ease and did not hesitate to explain the facts.

In many African tribes, I am informed, the chief is told only what he wants to hear; he is not told unpleasant facts if he prefers not to hear them. Only when he gives clear signs that always and under all circumstances he desires full information will he be told everything. This widespread cultural phenomenon is quite understandable, but it does not correspond to the Christian concept of frankness. Gradual communication of a serious diagnosis, especially of terminal illness, can be an excellent way to show love and truthfulness in a dynamic process of interpersonal relationships and constant openness. But it is simply unacceptable to tell lies only because some patients are not ready here and now for the full truth or because they have not been helped to prepare themselves properly.

Think of what would happen if doctors and members of the family followed the principle, "You should tranquilize the patient by means of lies as long as possible." There would be no way to free the patient from disbelief and suspicion. Even the most favorable diagnosis would not be accepted, and communication would be more and more meaningless.

In recent years, almost every country has discussed the advisability of human transplants: the transfer of healthy organs — from a person who has just died — to ailing people in need of them. Legislators who weigh this situation have to choose between two possibilities: either to allow doctors to make life-saving use of organs of the deceased as soon as death is certain (unless there is explicit protest by a last will or by family members) or to invite people — by way of their last wills — to donate their organs for use after their death.

The second possibility seems the more ideal if indeed a sufficient number of people thus generously extend — beyond their death — their responsibility for the life and health of others by donating the use of their organs. But I also see no serious objection to the first possibility when this concurs with public opinion and actually helps to save more lives.

Prayer

We praise you and thank you, Lord Jesus Christ, for having conquered sin-solidarity through your death and Resurrection and for having inducted all who believe in you into saving-solidarity, which gives a new meaning to the death of believers. We thank you for having done everything to free us from the law of anguish-filled death.

Each time we participate in the Eucharistic Sacrifice we praise and proclaim your death and Resurrection until you come, through Brother Death, to conduct us into the eternal kingdom of the Father.

We pray for the grace to persevere in your love, and we ask for a good death for ourselves and for all people, so that we finally can confide our lives into your hands.

Holy Mary, Mother of God, pray for us sinners, now and at the hour of our death.

17
MAINTAIN THE ENVIRONMENT

So God created man in his own image; in the image of God he created him; male and female he created them. God blessed them and said to them, "Be fruitful and increase, fill the earth and subdue it, rule over the fish in the sea, the birds of heaven, and every living thing that moves upon the earth." God also said, "I give you all plants that bear seed everywhere on earth, and every tree bearing fruit which yield seed: they shall be yours for food. All green plants I give for food to the wild animals, to all the birds of heaven, and to all reptiles on earth, every living creature." So it was; and God saw all that he had made, and it was very good.

Then the LORD God planted a garden in Eden away to the east, and there he put the man whom he had formed. The LORD God made trees spring from the ground, all trees pleasant to look at and good for food; and in the middle of the garden he set the tree of life and the tree of the knowledge of good and evil (Genesis 1:27-31, 2:8-9).

Forty years ago nobody would have expected in a book about morality in everyday living a chapter on ecological responsibility; only a new world situation and new knowledge have brought this dimension to the foreground. It has become a central problem of human and Christian responsibility in and for the world.

This does not imply, however, that in this area we have nothing to learn from Christians of the past. Remember Saint Francis of Assisi and his loving respect for animals and plants, the sun and the moon. He discovered in them a loving word of the Father in heaven; they invited him to see them as part of the great choir of praise to God. In

Saint Alphonsus' beautiful book *The Art of Loving Jesus,* the first part, "Love Calls for Love," relates how he admires a God who reveals his beauty and goodness and speaks to us his language of loving care for all of created reality. And he quotes many saints who understood the "language" of the world around them as a constant invitation to love and to praise God not only with fine words but also through a right attitude toward all creation.

The saints combine the spirit of praise and of reverence for God's gifts with a temperance that prevents them from idolizing creatures or becoming slaves of them. This basic attitude is more effective in the long run than mere principles and laws for the protection of ecological balance.

If the world of today would return to the spirit of praise found in the Psalms, in the whole Bible, and in all true disciples of Christ, it would not be too difficult to resolve the ecological crisis we speak of here. Through all these means we have been taught a redeemed and redeeming relationship with all of creation, together with a saving-solidarity with all of humankind in our own times and in generations to come.

The two accounts of creation in the first two chapters of Genesis are highly relevant for the right understanding of the relation between humankind and nature. Both accounts speak of God's loving care for his privileged human creature, but they also tell of his joy in all created reality and his solicitude for all living creatures.

God has given us no right to feel entitled to exploit nature. His will is that our attitude toward the environment is to be similar to his. As images of him, we want his creation to be and to remain "very good." We are to "subdue" the earth as faithful stewards of the Creator.

By entrusting the wondrous Garden of Eden to our first parents, God does indeed show great confidence in them; but he gives them no right whatsoever to act arbitrarily or ruthlessly with other creatures. If we entrust ourselves to God and accept his clear guidance to revere him in the celebration of the Sabbath and to continually worship him in all our divine and human relationships, then we surely will not lack a spirit of discernment and responsibility toward his environment.

Some modern writers try to blame not only Christians and Christendom for reckless treatment of the human environment but even divinely inspired Holy Scripture. To this end, they distort the word "subdue," taking it out of context and reading into the text an orientation toward a one-sided "doctrine of domination."

It is true that the prevailing "doctrine of domination" and the exploitation of nature in modern science, technology, economics, and politics are main causes of the sad ecological situation. It can also be agreed that Holy Scripture favored a sensible attitude toward the material world, the plants and animals, and contributed partially to the development of modern science and technology in the Western World. To combine a sensible attitude with a meaningful doctrine of domination is good; but to put the doctrine of domination and control in the first place and to neglect the doctrine of wholeness and salvation is bad. If the modern world has taken this course, it has been contrary to what Scripture and the lives of the saints have taught us and are still teaching us.

The God of the Bible is the Creator who blesses his work and teaches humanity about the preeminence of salvation truth and salvation knowledge. This includes the responsibility of humankind for the wholeness of persons, for good human relationships and care for a healthy world.

Even after the first sin, and, later, when the world was flooded with sins and sinful ways, God took care not only of the just man, Noah, and his descendants but also of all the species of animals, the pure and the so-called "impure." It is true that, in accord with the covenant with Noah, people are now entitled to eat the meat of animals — but with the condition that they imitate God in the preservation of the animal world (see Genesis 7 to 9).

Today's Christians, who take seriously the mission that they are "salt to the world," should properly inform themselves about the complex ecological problems in order to exercise their influence responsibly and to make their contribution toward shaping public opinion and important political decisions in this area.

Qualities We Must Have

There are three qualities necessary if Christians are to have a healthy impact on ecological problems. First, they have to be *adorers in spirit and truth;* second, they should be *gifted with wisdom and discernment;* third, they should be *creative in an affirmative sense.* This creativity allows for prudent manipulation of the given material of one's environment. We do not encroach on the limits of our mandate to subdue the earth when we unfold the dynamics of the biological and other processes or when we use our knowledge and skill to transform them in a way that helps people and harms no one.

We could never have our gardens, our agriculture, our capacity to feed six billion people without selective breeding, without irrigating arid land. We do well to thin out the forests in proper proportion and to multiply the harvest by chemical fertilizer. We are worthy of praise when we lay out wonderful parks and gardens; for even after the Fall it remains true that God has entrusted the earth to us as a wonderful garden. He put Adam ''in the garden of Eden to till it and to care for it'' (Genesis 2:15). Nothing can be said against our skill and planning in mining minerals used for the many purposes of economy and art. But all this has to be done with wisdom and care, so that the harmony of innumerable ecological factors which make for a healthy life will not be destroyed.

Today's highly developed scientific and technological people keep coming ever closer to limits which may not be exceeded without endangering our spaceship, Earth. And if our planet becomes uninhabitable, the fault would be with them. No powerful nation and no ''elite group'' of scientists and technologists have the right to take risks which might have deleterious effects on the whole of humankind and make all future generations suffer greatly. Irreversible mistakes can be made by unwise pioneering in an area where the complex interplay of various factors is not yet known to us.

The earth is part of an interaction between the sun and all the planets, and the sun system itself moves and develops in a not-yet-well-known interplay with all the other factors of the universe. On earth, billions of factors in the most complex interplay constitute the biosphere, the milieu of human life.

This interaction has already been seriously disturbed by recent developments: for instance, the waste of irreplaceable minerals, especially fossil energy resources, and by pollution of water and air. Billions of fish, destined by the Creator to reproduce themselves for all generations, die because of water pollution and as a result of various poisons from industrial wastes. The margin of tolerance of ionizing radiation by industry and armaments has been exceeded in many parts of the world. Asbestos is produced and used in increasing quantities, although it is now known as a principal cause of cancer, second only to excessive smoking.

The recent amazing progress in research of recombinant DNA might be a blessing in the field of medicine and genetics; it might open new horizons for selective breeding of plants, cereals, animals, and so on; but it might also produce irresistable viruses and endanger the genetic heritage.

Questions We Must Ask

The most threatening aspect in this whole situation, however, is that today's world has invested its energies one-sidedly in the doctrine of domination and exploitation, while permitting itself a shocking lapse of development in wisdom and discernment. Can humanity face the ecological crisis with any confidence if this disproportion continues?

The highly developed technologies of countries in both the East and the West are the main causes of the disturbed biosphere and ecosphere. If the countries of the so-called Third World were to encourage the same quantitative growth mania and excessive waste in consumption and armaments, humanity would be close to a total ecological collapse.

The main culprits and profiteers in this picture of ecological damage are also the outspoken enemies of a worldwide effort to raise people's awareness of the situation and to form an ecological conscience. A host of scientists, employed by the armament industries and their allies, seem set on deceiving the people who are becoming aware of the grave ecological dangers.

Yet, must not many of us ask ourselves, sincerely and humbly, if we are not somehow among the culprits? Are we ready to examine and eventually to change our consumer habits, our proneness to all kinds of waste? Have we that sound relationship with created reality which is based on adoration of God in spirit and truth? Are we willing to take our share of responsibility to promote a radical change of public opinion and life-style?

Who does not see that these questions have much to do with the universal vocation to holiness? With our personal vocation? The world is badly in need of saints; there are so many blind guides leading the blind! The world needs vocal prophets, not just verbal protesters.

This new asceticism beckons us not to corporal punishment but to a new kind of fasting, renunciation, and temperance as part of a life-style marked by simplicity and the joys inherent in it. And to form our conscience in this area we need an alert and competent ecological awareness combined with that creativity which discovers vital expressions of our new perceptions.

If we seek and cultivate joy in God, the spirit of adoration and praise, the inner peace and charism of peacemakers; if we cherish the final hope based on the divine promises and on the immense beauty we find in a healthy environment; if we continue to pray more for wisdom than for success, power, and wealth, then we will no longer feel the need for so many things that our wasteful culture induces us to want. And when parents begin to give themselves and their genuine love to their children, they will no longer need to give them the thousand useless or unnecessary things as substitutes for the missing love. Thus the children, too, will develop in a healthier environment.

Whoever clearly and sincerely faces the ecological problems of today's and tomorrow's world will see most of these moral questions in a new light.

Prayer

Lord Jesus Christ, you came here on earth to adore the Father, in the name of all humanity and all creatures, by the full truth of life, and thus to teach us "adoration in spirit and truth." Open our eyes, our hearts, and our minds to see, with you, the beauty and destiny of creation. From now on, we promise to become more aware that all things are created in you, the Eternal Word, and that you have taken the flesh of the earth to redeem the world. We want to thank you by our lives for having taught us to nurture healthy relationships among all people and to appreciate the gifts entrusted to our stewardship.

Help us, O Lord, to strive more for wisdom, knowledge of salvation, and discernment than for power and wealth. Help us to fulfill our firm purpose to administer our earthly heritage in solidarity with the poor and in responsibility for future generations.

Enlighten the men and women who have special competence in problems concerning the human biosphere and ecosphere. Guide with your wisdom those who have to make grave decisions in the economic and political realm. Help them to face realistically all ecological problems and to resolve them wisely in cooperation with all people of good will.

We cannot hope for a radical change and a healthy ecological future without conversion. So we pray: Lord, forgive us our sins against your creation, against the earth and the future generations; forgive our coveting more possessions, our mania for more consumption. And forgive us our cowardly silence in the face of all the dangerous delusions of our culture.

18
PROMOTE CHRISTIAN CULTURE

[Jesus said:] It is like a man going abroad, who called his servants and put his capital in their hands; to one he gave five bags of gold, to another two, to another one, each according to his capacity. Then he left the country. The man who had five bags went at once and employed them in business, and made a profit of five bags, and the man who had the two bags made two. But the man who had been given one bag of gold went off and dug a hole in the ground, and hid his master's money. A long time afterwards their master returned, and proceeded to settle accounts with them. The man who had been given the five bags of gold came and produced the five he had made: "Master," he said, "you left five bags with me; look, I have made five more." "Well done, my good and trusty servant!" said the master. "You have proved trustworthy in a small way; I will now put you in charge of something big. Come and share your master's delight" (Matthew 25:14-21).

Our history as human beings flows from nature and culture. Essentially, we are cultural beings, enabled and enriched by culture and devoted to culture. Surely, then, all of us should invest the talents we have received from God and make them profitable for ourselves, our neighbors, and future generations by promoting a culture that favors healthy personal relationships, growth of creative liberty and fidelity, and arrangement of the environment that actualizes truth, goodness, and beauty.

The proper realm of culture is not only the direct cult of beauty and the artistic expression of the great dimensions of human life; it also includes the shape of the landscape, the style of living, the decoration of one's home. As we have just seen, one of the greatest achievements of culture is a responsible attitude toward the milieu, the whole arrangement of the environment in view of the health and wholeness of persons and communities.

The arrangement and development of economic structures, processes, and dynamics in view of justice and peace should be among our greatest skills, although we frequently fail here because we lack a vision of wholeness which is the heart of all cultural endeavors. Good home management, totally ordered to the welfare of the family, requires wisdom and competence on the part of husbands and wives. Our management of national and international economics is extremely significant because of its enormous impact on the lives of millions of people: their human relationships, their value clarifications, and their endeavors for peace.

Christians who feel they are called to work in these areas of culture, economics, or politics and who possess the vision of wholeness and the necessary qualities of character — as well as the necessary competence to serve the common good, justice, and peace — are surely among the faithful servants to whom the Lord and Giver of talents promises a place at the festive board when the great day of accounting has arrived.

Gratitude for Our Heritage

Our dedication to the promotion of culture in its various areas and dimensions should be an expression of gratitude for our God-given talents, our cultural inheritance, and our eagerness to serve the present and future generations. There is so much to be grateful for! Think of all the practical knowledge contained in the many languages — including our own — the traditions, customs, wise laws, and countless masterpieces of art in which deep reflections and insights about the problems of life are embodied.

But all this does not help us and those who will follow us if we do not make individual and collective efforts to appreciate, understand, interiorize, and vitalize it in order to adapt it to present circumstances. The teacher of the moral law, and everyone who wants to fulfill his or her role in the on-going history of salvation, has to be "like a householder who can produce from his store both the new and the old" (Matthew 13:52).

In the face of changing situations, needs, and possibilities, it is the outstanding moral and religious leaders — those prophets and saints who discover new values or different ways to actualize traditional values — who are among the greatest promoters of culture. And they do this by establishing a perfect balance between the old and the new. Even though no artwork of theirs will ever appear in future museums, their work in helping human persons to reach the peaks of human culture will stand as a priceless masterpiece.

Those of us who have no expertise in any specific art can, nevertheless, be great artists if we truly become an image of God in love, justice, peace, and ennobling human relationships. Living according to our faith, open to all values, exercising discernment, remaining faithful to our conscience, and searching always for truth, goodness, and realistic solutions to our problems, we make a rich contribution to culture without explicitly thinking in terms of it.

When we consider the immense relevance of culture in all its dimensions and when we recognize what it can do for the well-being and dignity of all men and women, each of us — in accord with our own capabilities — should give explicit attention to the promotion of culture, so that its positive benefits are shared with all people, especially the poor.

In order to make a realistic contribution in this area we should first examine our society and its culture; then we should try to discern what benefits human persons and healthy relationships and what harms them. Our mission to be "light for all the world" and "salt to the world" will also demand from us a critical evaluation of our culture as well as a diligent pursuit of the best possible ways to contribute to sound public opinion, which is such an important dimension of culture.

The Church and Culture

It is an undeniable fact that in the course of history religion has made great contributions to the promotion of culture in almost all fields. The cultural productiveness of faith depends very much on how much the joy of faith influences the work of genius. Orthodoxy and piety alone are not enough. The faithful Christian must also mobilize the creative capacities entrusted to him or her for the benefit of all. The believer's irreplaceable contribution is a vision of wholeness, vigilance for the signs of the times, and a convincing embodiment of faith in his or her daily life.

One of the basic models for Christian involvement in culture is the Incarnation of the Word of God. Born an Israelite, Jesus, the God-Man, grew up in that culture. He owed his range of thought, his use of language, and his vision of history to the tradition of his people. The best of that culture, marked by God experience and by prophetic actualization, came to its fullness in him, the Son of man, the Son of God. He did not originate all the religious and moral values which he lived and proclaimed in a totally new way. Rather, he incorporated all the treasures of the religious and moral culture of Israel into his own unique mission in the fullness of time.

Jesus did not allow the Jewish culture to monopolize his thinking — not even in its religious dimensions. He often praised the faith of people who did not belong to that culture. The apostle to the Gentiles explained this in view of the common calling of both Jews and Gentiles to the new covenant in Christ. Man-made barriers have to be removed so that the good in all cultures can be appreciated and brought into this wholeness. "All that is true, all that is noble, all that is just and pure, all that is lovable and gracious, whatever is excellent and admirable — fill all your thoughts with these things" (Philippians 4:8).

Faithful to his mission, Paul can say: "To Jews I became like a Jew, to win Jews; as they are subject to the Law of Moses, I put myself subject to it. To win Gentiles, who are outside the Law, I made myself like one of them, although I am not in truth outside God's law. . . . Indeed, I have become everything in turn to men of every sort. . . . All this I do for the sake of the Gospel'' (1 Corinthians 9:20-22). ''I am under obligation to Greek and non-Greek, to learned and simple'' (Romans 1:13).

The Second Vatican Council, in its treatment of newly established communities of the faithful, insists that the Church must be incarnated in the various cultures so that ''the Christian life will be adapted to the mentality and character of each culture'' (*Missionary Activity,* 22). And a constant effort to do likewise must also be made, even in old established communities where a new culture is evolving. The spirit of evangelical poverty requires that we no longer cling to traditional forms where this would tarnish the newness of life in Christ and our mission to be ''salt to the world.'' Christians are to be neither the last ones to accept a new culture nor the first blind followers of the new only because it is new.

If faith is deeply rooted in the hearts and minds of all Christians, then, in faithful vigilance for the signs of the times, they will use to the full their present opportunities to make their approach to the various cultures and subcultures creative and redemptive. When we fully appreciate all the good in our own and in other cultures, and when we blend this appreciation with our full vision of faith and wholeness, we become better able to face the blemishes of our own culture, to purify what needs to be purified, and to oppose what contradicts human dignity. Thus, for example, Christians who live in a culture inclined to violence and force will give particular attention to nonviolence and nonviolent methods to solve conflicts. In an unculture of greed, intemperate consumerism, and wastefulness they will cultivate generosity in their dealings with the poor and simplicity in their own life-styles.

Prayer

We praise you, Father, Lord of heaven and earth, for having given to humankind such admirable capacities to cultivate the earth, to till the garden you have entrusted to us, and to care for it. You have given skill to craftsmen and have gifted many with a sense of beauty in their pursuit of the higher arts. Song and music are your gifts and people's joy. Above all, we thank you for having called us all to be co-artists with you as we strive to become masterpieces of goodness, love, peace, wisdom, and beauty.

We thank you for the rich cultural heritage of our nation and of all peoples, for the unique opportunity in our era when cultures can enrich each other and cultivate unity in variety as well as variety in unity. Let all feel that gratitude can be best expressed by creative fidelity and responsibility in consideration for present and future generations.

Assist your Church throughout the world to remain faithful to the momentous occurrence of the first Pentecost and to proclaim the Gospel in all languages to all cultures. Free Christians everywhere, but above all, in powerful nations, from any kind of cultural superiority complex. Lord, help us all to be faithful stewards in the promotion of Christian culture.

19
TRANSFORM THE ECONOMY

So I say to you, use your worldly wealth to win friends for yourselves, so that when money is a thing of the past you may be received into an eternal home.

The man who can be trusted in little things can be trusted also in great; and the man who is dishonest in little things is dishonest also in great things. If, then, you have not proved trustworthy with the wealth of this world, who will trust you with the wealth that is real? And if you proved untrustworthy with what belongs to another, who will give you what is your own?

No servant can be the slave of two masters; for either he will hate the first and love the second, or he will be devoted to the first and think nothing of the second. You cannot serve God and Money (Luke 16:9-13).

Set your mind on God's kingdom and his justice before everything else, and all the rest will come to you as well (Matthew 6:33).

For today's Christians — more so than for the first generation of Christ's disciples — active participation in economic life is imperative. This important decision is clearly based on a fundamental option: Only by setting our minds completely on God's kingdom and his saving justice can we arrive at true freedom in the economic realm and fulfill our liberating mission.

Once we have exercised our option to view economics under the banner of the Beatitudes we will gradually rid ourselves of our blindness, and begin to realize how frequently and how easily economic success and power are leagued with "unjust mammon," with sinful economic structures, and degrading exploitation and relationships.

As Christians we will not bait the whole economic system, like the Qumran sect did around the time of Jesus, but we should be leaders in the flight from all complicity with greed or the reckless striving for wealth and economic power that is so detrimental to the majority of people. Our flight, however, will not constitute a betrayal of our mission to be "salt to the world" and "salt" also to socioeconomic life.

Our flight from greed and the idolatry of wrongful economic values will free us to participate in creative and constructive measures to improve the economy. This is a prerequisite for being "light for all the world." "Be very sure of this: no one given to fornication or indecency, or the greed which makes an idol of gain, has any share in the kingdom of Christ and of God" (Ephesians 5:5).

I am afraid that those Christians who "make an idol of gain" while insisting on a severe sexual morality do not realize that they are as accountable for their particular sin as those who are "given to fornication and indecency." And if they persist in their ways, they cannot "have a share in the kingdom of Christ and of God." I think that the delusion still most common to men and women is that of Christians who are given to greed in its various forms and, alas, with a conscience that they call "good."

Modern Economic Systems

The modern development of economics is, from one point of view, a huge success; it manages to feed more than four billion people. Most citizens of the highly industrialized nations live abundant lives. But modern economics has also failed miserably in the matter of just distribution. So many millions of people live in misery, suffering starvation as Lazarus did at the threshold of the rich reveler. The sad reason is that, since the rise of capitalism, economic life is crowded with sinister idols and ideologies in both the East and the West.

For many people, economic activity is governed exclusively by motives of material success, efficiency, wealth, and power. Classical liberalism advanced an ideology which would justify this approach and at the same time leave the successful with a good conscience. It taught that the economic realm has to develop according to its own dynamics and incentives and should not be harassed by moral imperatives. It promised that individualism would guarantee the best possible success and allow for the interplay of supply and demand.

Many who call themselves Christians have followed this same reasoning, at least in practice. And if, by some chance, they become uneasy of conscience, they try to quiet and console it by almsgiving and pious or humanitarian philanthropies. Thus they would pay a kind of modest tithing from the profits gathered by an unjust mammon under an unjust economic system which allows heartless exploitation of the weak.

Classical Marxism adopted from this liberalism the ideology of autonomy in the economic realm; it added, however, some new and particularly dangerous dimensions. In Marxism, the economy not only makes its own iron laws of dynamics and processes but it also provides the determining factor for the whole of social life. It is true that Marxism disapproves of individualism — not for moral reasons but because of its attitude toward private property. It rejects an ethical foundation of socialism, since inherent to its ideology of socioeconomic life is class war and class hatred as the dynamic of historical development. In the existing systems of Marxism the machinery of state-capitalism functions even more heartlessly than capitalism with its private ownership of productive capital.

Both of these ideologies have espoused the evil of reckless armament, now made possible because of technical and economic expansion. These explosive risks are magnified by the theory and practice of class wars, in which the "real Marxism" in power combines ruthless oppression of the worker class with war between the classes and war against other systems.

It is still true, however, that, even with the bad effects of "unjust mammon," some important social advantages have been made possible by the free enterprise system and by some socialist states. In many countries insurance is available for the time of sickness and unemployment, and security is provided for workers after retirement; and in some countries, employees have been given more say in the decision-making process and a better share in the business profits. Considerable, but still insufficient, efforts are being made to humanize labor.

Christians know from experience that the effects of original sin or "sin of the world" are present in the economic realm; they recognize the prejudice of economic systems which, in theory and practice, prevent workers from securing economic freedom. Economic greed has shaped harmful structures confirmed by no less harmful ideologies. Promoted through the powerful channels of the mass media, bizarre commandments are being insinuated: Thou shalt covet; thou shalt buy more; thou shalt consume more; thou shalt flaunt thy wealth!

As Christians, of course, we know that Jesus came to redeem all people, regardless of their ideologies. It therefore behooves us to encourage all efforts for more justice, unselfishness, moderation, and freedom from strife as signs of hope for redemption and liberation. We must directly oppose dangerous economic idols and ideologies, but at the same time we should keep our eyes and hearts open to welcome any efforts directed toward an authentic culture in the economic realm.

We all realize that unjust and unhealthy economic structures favor sinful and criminal practices; but instead of blaming all economic evils on structures — thus practically excusing the culprits — we must treat this widespread criminality in economic life as an ethical question. True, these structures have to be changed; but while we seek the necessary social remedies, we need to alert the entire community about the importance of change.

Empirical studies show the shocking extent of unethical and criminal conduct in business. Some managers and owners conduct their business on the basis of borderline morality; and then they consistently lower their standards. Meanwhile, powerful groups in industry and business use means — often unfair — to block legislation which would set a minimum of legally required standards of honesty and justice.

The fundamental problem here is that too many people do not trouble themselves to act ethically. It seems their only concern is to avoid conflict with penal laws. They are willing to be "honest" only insofar as this promises more for their profit-oriented business activity. We can only hope that the majority of employees, executives, and managers can be counted more or less among those whom the Lord praises as faithful servants (see Luke 16:9-12). Christians can be "salt to the world" in the economic realm only if they are absolutely honest and reliable, even when this requires sacrifices and creates disadvantages.

Yet in today's world even this is not enough. Each and every one of us, through wise and courageous cooperation, ought to do what we can to improve society in general and the economic culture in particular, beginning in our own homes and continuing with the promotion of a new economic world order. For this purpose we need to study the social doctrines of the Church and all other promising leads. Here, too, we need knowledge, competence, cooperation, and the ever-necessary good will.

Our Christian Goals

The enormous tasks in this field can be faced only by solidly united and competent Christians cooperating with all people of good will. Here are some important goals to keep in mind:

● Application of the basic principles of social justice;

- A worldwide solidarity, especially among all who participate in economic life;
- Subsidiarity which requires the highest possible level of sharing in decision-making processes concerning people's own well-being and that of the powerless;
- Justice to the aging and retired;
- Effective application of equal dignity and equal rights for women in professional and industrial life;
- Fair and generous cooperation between the highly industrialized, wealthy countries and the poverty-stricken developing nations.

Those who earn their money honestly must not be content to stand aside, as if their example alone will influence others to be honest. No, if they have the proper discernment and know-how to instill this sense of justice in others, it is important that they do so. Our call to salvation and holiness is essentially a call to mission, *action,* "to be salt to the world."

Some excuse themselves by saying that nothing can be changed for the better. This pessimism is, in reality, a denial of the message that the Lord's redemption is plentiful. It presumes to deny Christ as Savior of the entire world, and leans perilously close to a narrow image of him as "Savior only of souls." Of course redemption is also a matter of saving one's soul; but those who do not intend to cooperate in the salvation of people in all their dimensions and relationships, who do not accept their vocation to improve society as a whole, also destroy their own souls.

The affirmation of one's own co-responsibility for the improvement of community life, including the economic realm, is intimately connected with the decisive criteria which the Savior and Judge of the world indicated for the Day of Judgment (see Matthew 25:31-46). By working with others to improve community life we can heal and even prevent many wounds; and in this way we capably perform the works of mercy and saving justice of which the Gospel speaks.

Private charity, important though it is, cannot substitute for one's grave neglect of cooperation for a better ordering of the economic life which — in its present bad shape — inflicts so many wounds, makes so many people lonely prisoners of "the system," submits countless people to hunger and starvation, and deprives many of decent care, clothing, and housing.

By the way we live and in various other ways we have become a part of these unjust and harmful economic structures and activities. We need conversion. But individual conversion, which always takes precedence, implies more than personal disengagement. What is needed is that all those converted and those on the road to conversion should work in solidarity for a profound change in our economic culture (unculture?) and ask themselves and each other questions like the following.

Some Questions

- Are we willing to free ourselves and others from the still-prevailing ideology of quantitative growth (growth mania) and offer instead concrete, realistic, and, at the same time, idealistic ways to qualitative growth?
- Are we willing to give concrete evidence that alternative ways of simple life-styles are possible and even attractive?
- Are we willing to give personal witness that a moderate use of material goods brings more happiness and peace than wastefulness and greed?
- Are we willing to help each other to read the signs of the times and to acknowledge that the present trend to ever-greater wastefulness of irreplaceable resources of energy and rare raw materials can no longer continue without grave injustice to future generations and even to our own generation?
- Are we willing to remind wealthy people and rich nations that the poorest people and nations have a legitimate claim to a rightful share of the earth's goods?
- Should we not combine with convincing life-styles the art of dialogue to influence public opinion in this area?

If we lack the courage and creative initiative to take these steps, we have to wonder whether our faith in redemption, our faith in the Redeemer of the world, is sufficiently alive.

It is true that, at best, we are only in the initial stages of conversion and have only begun to formulate solidly united actions of renewal. What we need, then, is a well-defined goal and a concerted effort to seek each day the proper means to establish a balanced socioeconomic order — an economy that serves real needs instead of creating artificial and harmful ones, a better balance of work and leisure time (to reduce unemployment), and an economic system that encourages creativity and joy on the part of workers.

The Sermon on the Mount does not provide us with a concrete model for today's economic systems; it offers no panacea for resolving the increasing danger of worldwide conflict. But it does give us clear directions for the attitudes which believers need in order to be "light for all the world," attitudes which will serve as a firm foundation in our sincere search for ways and means to reach our Christian goals.

In order to pledge ourselves to the radical conversion described in this chapter, we need to "beatitudinize" our economic system.

Beatitudes of Economy

Where people believe in the kingdom of God and concentrate on God's saving justice above all, there the weak and poor no longer are degraded and exploited.

Where disciples of Christ hunger and thirst for God's justice, there the greed for more money and more power over others fades away.

Where believers practice Christ's gentleness, there will be found a solution to conflicts.

Where people faithfully and gratefully praise the God of mercy, there will be no class hatred, no group selfishness, and no neglect of the handicapped.

Where believers' hearts are purified by embracing God's love,

there will grow a sympathetic understanding of people's genuine needs.

Where men and women consider themselves highly blessed and honored to be called children of God, there will be total commitment to peace, justice, and reconciliation.

Where people truly believe the message of the Gospel, there will be brave souls like Bishop Romero of El Salvador and thousands of others who are ready to suffer persecution and death for the sake of authentic peace and saving justice. And despite temporary lack of success, they will not lose hope for they have entrusted themselves to God.

All this is an essential part of our Christian calling and mission: "You are salt to the world."

The message of the Sermon on the Mount to "put away anxious thoughts about food and drink" and the invitation to look at the "birds of the air" and "the lilies . . . in the fields" are in no way a call to withdraw from public life and pursue our own selfish interests. Rather, these words call us to the all-encompassing mission to set our minds on God's kingdom before all else (see Matthew 6:25-34).

Amazing things could happen in the realm of economics, culture, and politics if we Christians would believe the Gospel with all our hearts. Then, as people renewed by this spirit, we would determine definite ways and means to make the Gospel a reality. E. F. Schumacher, a fine expert in the field of economics, is convinced that this is what the world needs above all else.

Prayer

Lord Jesus Christ, you designated yourself as "bread for the life of the world." You lived and died for others, and you taught us to ask the Father for our daily bread, the bread which unites all people. Convert us by the power of your Spirit so that, as a community dedicated to mutual service, we may begin the task of arranging our socioeconomic relationships in a way that respects the treasures of the earth and the fruit of our labor as gifts from the one Father of us all.

Lord, deliver workers and business people from greed and division. Help us also to discover your design for salvation in the area of economics. Grant us wisdom and courage to work for the healing of economic structures, suffering from wounds of greed and lust for power. Give the world saints who show us what it really means to believe in you as the Savior of the world.

God, Father of us all, let the world perceive in us people whose primary purpose is to honor your name, to pray for and to experience the coming of your kingdom. Teach us to seek your will in all things, to help provide bread for all your children. May we learn from your generous and healing actions to unite with others in an effort to remedy the appalling conditions which prevail today on the world's economic front. Above all, renew our faith in your plentiful redemption so that we will firmly commit ourselves to the liberation of all men and women from the enormous evil that besets our world.

20
EXERT POLITICAL INFLUENCE

Jesus answered him [the devil], "Scripture says again, 'You are not to put the Lord your God to the test.'"

Once again, the devil took him to a very high mountain, and showed him all the kingdoms of the world in their glory. "All these", he said, "I will give you, if you will only fall down and do me homage." But Jesus said, "Begone, Satan! Scripture says, 'You shall do homage to the Lord your God and worship him alone.'"

Then the devil left him; and angels appeared and waited on him (Matthew 4:7-11).

Every person must submit to the supreme authorities. There is no authority but by act of God, and the existing authorities are instituted by him; consequently anyone who rebels against authority is resisting a divine institution, and those who so resist have themselves to thank for the punishment they will receive. For government, a terror to crime, has no terrors for good behavior. You wish to have no fear of the authorities? Then continue to do right and you will have their approval, for they are God's agents working for your good. But if you are doing wrong, then you will have cause to fear them; it is not for nothing that they hold the power of the sword, for they are God's agents of punishment, for retribution on the offender. That is why you are obliged to submit. It is an obligation imposed not merely by fear of retribution but by conscience. That is also why you pay taxes. The authorities are in God's service and to these duties they devote their energies.

Discharge your obligations to all men; pay tax and toll, reverence and respect, to those to whom they are due (Romans 13:1-7).

An idea of how much can be accomplished by good and capable politicians can be gleaned by examining the lives of such men as Robert Schuman, Alcide de Gasperi, and Konrad Adenauer. These Christian men of excellent political abilities negotiated with conviction and skill for the reconciliation of their nations and for European solidarity. In contrast to them, examine the stupidity of those who voted for Hitler in 1933 or entered into alliances with his party because of collective and personal selfishness; and consider also those who brought Stalin to power and sustained him in it. Think, too, of the millions of citizens who simply neglected their political responsibility and thus let evil prevail and perdure.

In the early Christian era, when the small minority of Christians could not even dream of exercising a positive influence in the political arena, simple people could do little more than quietly fulfill their civic duties and offer prayers ''for sovereigns and all in high office, that we may lead a tranquil and quiet life in full observance of religion and high standards of morality'' (1 Timothy 2:2). It was necessary that Christians be instructed on the meaning and limits of dutiful obedience to political rulers and civil laws.

Only in their overall view do the texts of the Bible offer a fairly clear direction in the area of politics. On the one hand, they affirm responsible obedience; on the other, they unmask and condemn abuse of political power.

Insistence on obedience is found especially in Paul's Letter to the Romans and in the first Letter of Peter. In the latter, it is evident that the main purpose of the text is to show that Christians were unjustly accused of being enemies of the Roman Empire, enemies of the state. ''Submit yourselves to every human institution for the sake of the Lord, whether to the sovereign as supreme, or to the governor as his deputy for the punishment of criminals and the commendation of those who do right. For it is the will of God that by your good conduct you should put ignorance and stupidity to silence'' (1 Peter 2:13-15).

There is also good reason to believe that our opening text from the Epistle to the Romans was intended to reassure the political powers that they have nothing to fear from Christians. But in both cases the evident concern is that Christians give their support to the common welfare by exemplary obedience to just laws made by political authorities. Paul's insistence that it is ''an obligation imposed not merely by fear of retribution but by conscience'' (Romans 13:5) indicates not only the kind of obligation but also its limits. Nobody is allowed to offer the state an obedience that is against an upright conscience.

The position of the early Church on political power was primarily critical. Jesus himself, *the* Prophet, continued and fulfilled the prophetic tradition which unmasked and chastized the abuse of power and any kind of exploitation and oppression of the weak and poor. If Jesus had spoken only of the salvation of souls, the leaders of Israel and the Roman authorities would have left him in peace. He expressed a candid characterization of Herod when he called him a ''fox'' (Luke 13:32).

Jesus vented his prophetic wrath at the appalling abuse of religious authority displayed by the leaders of the Jewish people. He knew that he was to become a victim of their diabolical plot arising from a mixture of religion and lust for power. And this saddened him because he recognized that they were being misled by their beliefs concerning an earthly Messianic arrival. His reaction to temptations (as recorded in Matthew 4:7-11) shows how shameless Jesus considered this kind of behavior and how sharply he opposed it.

His attitude becomes even more clear in his harsh correction of Peter when this privileged apostle, who had just acknowledged Jesus as the Messiah, demonstrated how he had been misled by an erroneous expectation of a Messiah who would dominate people by sheer power. Contaminated by this widespread error, Peter could not yet accept a meek, powerless, suffering ''servant-of-God.'' In this context Jesus even calls Peter a "Satan" and a "stumbling-block" (see Matthew 16:23).

As witnesses to the coming of God's kingdom, the disciples of Jesus are urged to develop attitudes directly opposed to those of kings and powerful men of this world (see Luke 22:24-27). If all Christians were to observe these directives, the great prophecies of the coming of God's kingdom would become more evident. Then the on-going power struggles among Christians and the insatiable hunger for privileges and lordly titles would finally be unmasked in their utter nonsense — all to the benefit of the political realm.

The history of humanity, even to the present day, is filled with erroneous and dangerous Messianic expectations, not the least of which is the new Israelitic state whose fate may yet depend upon this consideration. With sadness, we recall the appalling theory of Boniface VIII and others regarding the "two swords of the church"; all the "holy" wars; the wars of the Spanish crown against the South American Indians who were not ready to accept Baptism; the wars of aggression waged by the early English Protestant colonizers against the North American aborigines. All these were based on an erroneous concept of "chosenness" in preference to others.

History records numerous examples of this in the secular field: leaders who designated their states as "chosen nations" in the political and economic wars of Europe. A sad example of this was the case of American politicians who insisted on "unconditional surrender" of the Germans and Japanese, leading — in the latter case — to what was called "moral justification" for the use of atom bombs against open cities in Japan. There are also the apartheid politics in South Africa; and, last but not least, Hitler's holocaust in excuse for his myth of a "chosen" race.

Historians also see, in the devious philosophy of the Kremlin's Marxism, a strange mixture of the Messianic ideas of Czarist Russia and the Slavic traditions on one hand and, on the other, the secularized Messianism of Karl Marx, who announced a golden age as a result of class struggle brought about by dialectic evolution.

Imperialism, militarism, and intolerance in their worst forms are the bitter fruits of various kinds of false religions and/or secularized ideologies of redemption. All this can be seen in its proper perspective when we hear Jesus cry out: "If only you had known, on this great day, the way that leads to peace!" (Luke 19:42)

Our Political Vocation

True disciples of Christ know that when they think and speak of "chosenness" (election), which flows from their call to holiness and their mission to be "light to the world," they can do so only because they are humble followers of the Prince of Peace, the Servant of God and humankind, Jesus Christ. This is what is most needed for the redemption of the political realm: Christians who truly live this vision of faith by their authentic witness and responsible activity.

The frequently quoted and often misunderstood words of Jesus, "Then pay Caesar what is due Caesar, and pay God what is due to God" (Matthew 22:21; Mark 12:17; Luke 20:25), should be understood in this sense: Steadfastly refuse to give the emperor divine worship, but submit to his authority in other matters. Whoever pays to God what is due to God, adoring him throughout life (see Matthew 4:10), will contribute to the common welfare but will never accord divine worship to sovereigns and states.

The New Testament texts that deal with moral obligations in the field of politics have to be read within this context. Christians are by no means anarchists; but, if they follow the great prophetic tradition culminating in Christ, they will never be submissive followers of dictators, imperialists, or militarists.

We should keep in mind the song of praise voiced by the humble handmaid, the Mother of Jesus, who is thoroughly marked by this prophetic vision: "The arrogant heart and mind he has put to rout, he has brought down monarchs from their thrones" (Luke 1:52). And the Book of Revelation, with its downright rejection of any form of cult bestowed on earthly power or on emperors, portrays the Church as a follower of Mary and the Servant-Messiah. She is a magnificent sign of salvation in contrast to the dragon with his "seven heads" and "seven diadems" (see Revelations 12:4).

Today's Christians must ask themselves whether they are actually manifesting this tension between creative loyalty and prophetic honesty in the realm of politics. If Christians realize the importance of skillful participation in the political arena and if they firmly believe in their vocation to holiness, then we can hope that the world will be blessed by men and women who are devout and competent political activists.

Holy Scripture informs us of the drastic tension between the original design of the Creator, the weakness of human nature after the fall from grace, and the fact of redemption. The decisive word is *redemption*. Believers, whose whole lives praise the gift of redemption, will discover gradually the design of the Creator and Redeemer and will be able to face the reality of original sin or "the sin of the world."

Power — especially absolute power — is exposed to the greatest temptations. History shows us that this is true of both political and religious powers. The organization of the Church and its exercise of religious authority should not be cast in the mold of political powers.

The Second Vatican Council emphasizes the "otherness" of the successors of the apostles. Their proclamation of the Gospel derives from "the power of God, who very often reveals the might of the Gospel through the weakness of its witnesses. For those who dedicate themselves to the ministry of God's Word should use means and helps proper to the Gospel. In many respects these differ from the supports of the earthly city" (*Church in the Modern World,* 76).

By fidelity to the Gospel, Christians — who are at the same time citizens of the earthly city and of the kingdom of God — are able to exercise great influence in exposing the temptations of power and in manifesting the ways of saving-solidarity. Christians do not engage the political power as such, but they will be on the alert for and will call attention to the pitfalls and temptations to which it is constantly exposed.

Necessary Means for Political Renewal

The battle against our individual and collective selfishness and against the different kinds of lust for power goes hand in hand with a creative effort for political renewal. Our fight against our personal sinfulness is inseparable from the fight against the "sin of the world," especially as it is manifested in abuse of power and authority. It should be remembered that the field of politics is a breeding ground for the "sin of the world" and that Christians — by their redemptive presence in this area — can do much to lessen the evil.

An intelligent and faithful application of the principle of subsidiarity on all levels is one of the most effective means to establish a proper balance of power. This fundamental principle of Catholic social ethics implies a widespread and organic distribution of power, whereby it is always subordinate to participation, service, and coresponsibility.

Individual initiative must not be hampered. What the family can do in a meaningful way should not be usurped by the political community. The purpose of family leadership is, above all, to strengthen the family's own functions. What can be done at the lower level should not be usurped by the higher level of political, social, or economic bodies. If urgent needs of the common welfare or evident inability (to perform the task) require higher authority to assume functions which would be performed ordinarily at a lower level, then every effort must be made to restore conditions which allow the lower level to perform the functions. All trends toward centralism must be considered abnormal at the moment they become opposed to subsidiarity.

If the principle of subsidiarity functions well on all levels — strengthening personal responsibility and guarding against appropriation of disproportionate power — then we will be able to favor and foster the development of a world authority without the otherwise justified fear that this might become perverted into an all-devouring Moloch of power.

Democratic Process

For these and other reasons, the social doctrine of recent popes has favored the spread of democracy, insofar as this is historically possible. We would describe an authentic democracy as a federation-type organization which maintains balanced distribution of power, observance of the principle of subsidiarity, and election — by the people — of representatives for only a specific length of time. Free elections at regular intervals must allow the people to give approval or disapproval, to give opportunities to other parties and coalitions, and to indicate the main principles of the desired programs.

Democracy is built on the principle of tolerance and free participation of all in the formation of public opinion. Of course, political tolerance does not extend to a group or party which intends to take absolute power and to deprive the majority of the people of their participation.

The proper functioning of democracy is unthinkable without a thorough political formation of all the people. No party or government should be allowed a monopoly in political formation, for this would imply manipulation in favor of a group reaching for permanent or absolute power.

Political formation involves the creation of a political conscience. Citizens must know about the values at stake in political decisions, and they must follow a scale of values by which they evaluate the decisions. A politically mature conscience knows the proper goals of political activity, the needs of the common welfare, and the need to explore, through shared responsibility, the best possible means to reach the right goals. In our wayward world it also implies a keen awareness of the dangers of individual and collective selfishness. There must be a constant effort for ever-better political achievement and a readiness for self-criticism by the individuals and groups involved. Yet, in striving toward this ideal system we must not forget that politics in an imperfect and wayward world always requires the "art of the possible."

When we vote, when we choose a particular political party, and when we play our part in the formation of public opinion, we must be constantly aware of the common welfare. We should never lose sight of our political ideals; however, realistically speaking, there will be times when we will have to choose the lesser of two evils — because the best is not available. As long as we continue to work in the right direction the "art of the possible" does not constitute a betrayal of conscience.

Prayer

Lord God, Father of us all, help us to perceive our political responsibility; teach us to recognize that political formation is a duty that we must not neglect. Grant us the gifts of wisdom and discernment.

Free us from the bonds of narrowness, from the chains of collective and individual selfishness. Grant us, along with love for our fatherland, a sense of global solidarity that prepares us to work with people all over the world.

Give us wise and competent men and women who have a genuine political vocation — people who are able to fulfill political roles in our communities, in our countries, and in international organizations.

21
SPREAD THE GOSPEL OF PEACE

Come, let us climb up on to the mountain of the LORD,
*   to the house of the God of Jacob,*
*   that he may teach us his ways*
*   and we may walk in his paths.*
For instruction issues from Zion
*   and out of Jerusalem comes the word of the LORD;*
*   he will be judge between nations,*
*   arbiter among many peoples.*
They shall beat their swords into mattocks
*   and their spears into pruning-knives;*
*   nation shall not lift sword against nation*
*   nor ever again be trained for war (Isaiah 2:3-4).*

Salt is a good thing; but if the salt loses its saltness, what will
you season it with?
Have salt in yourselves; and be at peace with one another
(Mark 9:50).

To ''have salt in'' ourselves means that we are permeated with the peace of the Lord and are prepared to be messengers of peace, to radiate peace. If we Christians, as individuals or as a community, lack peace, then our Christianity is without flavor. The peace for which Christ has come and which he has promised to his disciples is a blessed gift to everyone who truly believes in him and trusts in him. And whoever receives this gift gratefully will realize that it is a gift intended for all: one cannot be a possessor of peace without also being its messenger.

The peace of Christ is an indivisible, all-embracing gift. It is first experienced as peace with God; Paul describes it as keeping guard over our hearts and thoughts, in Christ Jesus (see Philippians 4:7). Since the Prince of Peace is the Liberator of the world from injustice, hatred, and war, no one can enjoy Christ's peace of heart without committing himself or herself to the mission of peace for all people.

Jesus' Peace Mission

Peace is the pivotal point of the prophetic expectation of Israel and even more so in the New Testament, which frequently is called simply "the Gospel of Peace." The "Shalom" of the risen Christ lifts his disciples from sadness and fills their hearts with joy and trust. And when he repeats his greeting using the same word, he gives them their mission of peace: "As the Father sent me, so I send you" (John 20:21). He breathes his peace into their hearts and grants them his Spirit whose fruits are "love, joy, peace" (see Galatians 5:22).

An essential part of the peace mission is the proclamation of forgiveness to all who need forgiveness (see John 20:23). The apostles of peace and reconciliation come as Christ's ambassadors (see 2 Corinthians 5:20), pleading for people to heed the hour of favor. And we all know that Jesus himself said that peacemakers will be called the sons and daughters of God (see Matthew 5:9).

The mission for peace is more than a superficial challenge. Their intimate appreciation of the gift of peace makes the disciples of Christ yearn for all people to experience it. They pray and dedicate themselves to the work of peace.

Christ, as is evident from Scripture, wants to make sure that his disciples are able to distinguish true peace — granted by him — from all false talk about peace. The one who brings peace does disturb people, rousing their consciences, making them aware that they are in need of proper reconciliation and genuine peace. This detachment from false and even unworthy peace is strongly symbolized in the action of Jesus when he drove from the temple those who would make religion a business (see Mark 11:15-17).

Those who desire the peace of Christ must separate themselves from any spirit of deception, greed, or lust for power. Christ himself knows that his message will bring him anguish (see Luke 12:50). His person and his message force people to make decisions which will be violently opposed by those who reject his peace (see Luke 12:51-53). The messengers of Christ's Gospel of peace will experience what the prophet Simeon foretold at Christ's coming into the world: "This child is destined to be a sign which men reject. . . . Many in Israel will stand or fall because of him" (Luke 2:35).

When we hear Jesus saying to his disciples, "Peace is my parting gift to you, my own peace, such as the world cannot give" (John 14:27), we recall the frequently used phrase at that time, *Pax Romana*. This was the so-called Roman peace, which was offered to those conquered by the sword and who showed themselves willing to accept colonial status. But the peace of Christ has nothing to do with the conquest of people by means of the sword. The Prince of the Messianic peace, exalted on the Cross, wants to draw people to himself and to the Father's kingdom by the power of his nonviolent love. This divine design of peace and salvation is a kind of two-edged sword. It forces our hearts to take sides for or against this peace.

Evidently, there were people in our Lord's time who misunderstood some of his words and actions. Jesus, the Lamb of God, meekly following the road to suffering and death, did not want his disciples to use the sword (see Matthew 26:52). Yet, in Matthew (10:34) Jesus says, "I have not come to bring peace but a sword." But Luke is more precise: "I have come to bring division" (Luke 12:51). Challenged by Christ, who is Peace in person, the hidden conflicts between light and darkness come into the open.

Those who still think that swords — or now even nuclear weapons — are the proper means for the reign of light should remember Jesus' abrupt response, "Enough, enough" (Luke 22:38), to his disciples' talk about swords. He was telling them that he wanted to hear no more talk about swords. It is shocking to hear how often people, who call themselves Christians, continue to talk quite readily about the ''two swords,'' confusing the sword of the word of God with the weaponry of unredeemed man.

Our Peace Mission

While Christians must unfailingly give witness to justice and peace, they must also be ready and eager to resolve conflicts by nonviolent means. This is a part of their mission that they cannot decline.

What every peace lover needs is a profound knowledge of Christ, the Prince of Peace, and a thorough appreciation of the peace which he grants. Such a one can then harmonize prophetic honesty with the patient and difficult art of nonviolent action in the struggle against deceit, exploitation, and injustice. Do we want to follow Christ in his courageous unmasking of hypocrisy and injustice? Then we must learn from him to suffer patiently and to forgive untiringly in our efforts to bring justice, truth, and peace to a world violently opposed to pacifism.

Mahatma Gandhi and Martin Luther King risked their lives and finally sacrificed them for *satyagraha,* a system of nonviolence which emphasized the power of truth, love, justice, and solidarity in the service of the downtrodden. Gandhi, though not formally a Christian, was a fervent disciple of Christ; he was convinced that this method embodied the central message of the Sermon on the Mount and the life and death of Christ.

In their *ashrams* (houses of prayer), the followers of Gandhi are trained in the use of *satyagraha*. They learn that it means nothing less than total dedication to the liberating truth that God is love and that he is a God of peace. They are confident that this liberating truth, when totally upheld throughout life, is more powerful than all the on-slaughts of evil.

This Ghandian method of achieving social and political reform relies on the art of detecting our inner forces of truth and love for ourselves and others (including our enemies), of regarding them as precious gifts of God, and activating them by unwavering love.

This will require of us the courage to eliminate our primitive patterns of hatred, our trust in menacing armaments, our classification of certain people as "cunning enemies" who fully deserve to be debased. In following this method we will need the inner strength and the necessary knowledge to say to our enemies, even the most threatening ones: "In you, too, there are forces that can be awakened for truth, justice, love, and peace."

At this moment of history when all the world has to choose between the dove of peace and the hawk of war, each family, each monastery, each parish, indeed the whole Church, should become an *ashram* — a house of prayer — where we allow the Divine Master to teach us, from within, the liberating truth of the power of the Gospel of peace. We need such houses of prayer where we can learn, in our day-by-day struggles with life, the art of healthy and healing relationships, of peaceful solution of conflicts. Only after constantly imploring this gift of peace from above will it take root in the hearts of all.

Satyagraha, as we have described it, must become the heart of our quest for peace and our development of peace throughout the world. We must create an atmosphere that frees us from thoughts of violence. Our words and actions are needed to promote freedom from greed, arrogance, lust for power, manipulation of persons, and any tendency to make people tools of our selfish purposes.

Importance of Nonviolence

It is my firm conviction that the only way we Christians can break out of the vicious circle of the armaments race is for all of us to take on the attitude of and apply the skill of *satyagraha*. This will be a concrete sign of our faith in the Gospel of peace, and it should become the most effective "defense contract" we ever made. It will be the "spiritual weaponry" of which Saint Paul speaks in his Epistle to the Ephesians, and will serve as our defense "against cosmic powers, against the authorities and potentates of this dark world."

Using God's armor, we must put on the "belt of truth," make morality our "coat of mail," the Gospel of peace the "shoes on . . . [our] feet." And with this "firm footing," we will meet the world with our "great shield of faith . . . [and] the sword which the Spirit gives" (Ephesians 6:12,14-17).

Any nation or system of government that still clings to the awful madness of imposing its will and collective selfishness on other systems and nations, by brutal threats of nuclear and chemical warfare, must be brought to its senses and convinced of its wrong by communities and nations who have taken up the nonviolent weaponry of *satyagraha*.

To heal those nations whose ills are caused by their ruthless ideologies we need other nations that are willing to withstand evil and solidly unite in the spirit and art of nonviolence. Would not the soldiers of oppressors and violent rulers be humbled and brought to reflection when they see the spiritual and moral power of nations and social groups who could challenge them to learn this "higher" art — the only real art in the battle for the reign of truth, justice, and abiding peace?

In today's world, this method of nonviolence is perhaps the best way we can give witness to our faith in Christ, the Prince of Peace. Christians should make a conscious effort to utilize this gift of Christ. Becoming leaders in this area, they will gratefully accept the witness of prophets like Gandhi.

All people who have the inner strength to choose *satyagraha* and the sacrifices entailed, all who cooperate untiringly with Christians and non-Christians and prepare themselves for its faithful practice, are sons and daughters of God. They have already opted for the Gospel of the peace of Christ, even though they may not be fully conscious of this supreme choice for the kingdom of God.

"You are light for all the world." This is our mission received from Christ. If humanity is to be saved from self-destruction, we Christians must give witness to the Gospel of peace by our life-styles, our love for fellow human beings, our attitude toward God's creatures, our wise and tolerant treatment of the ecology, our commitment to a qualitative (instead of a mere quantitative) growth of the economic life, and our political efforts to ensure the reign of peace.

In every aspect and phase of life we must help each other to cultivate peace and nonviolence, discovering together ever anew the beauty and resources of the Gospel of peace. There are numerous inventive ways to affirm, confirm, and spread our belief that peace is possible if we have true faith in the Prince of Peace. We should do whatever is in our power to strengthen this faith, realizing, of course, that peace is not possible without sacrifice on our part.

Mere passive pacifism, which stands clear of political controversy and other realities, will not do. As blessed peacemakers (Matthew 5:9), we must face the realities of life — right on the front line — in order to work for peace in a nonviolent way. As servants of peace we must be ready to give our all, without complaining and without losing our faith in the Gospel of peace.

Peace apostles will observe the political scene, fully aware of its complexity, and respond with the best possible competence, always ready to cooperate with all groups and individuals who believe in the possibility of peace. They will never tire in their efforts to transform all of politics into politics of peace. This means that always and everywhere the concern for peace and justice takes precedence.

People who unreservedly believe in the God of peace certainly realize that no person may exploit or degrade another person, and no group may exploit or degrade another group. If this is not a conviction which we pursue in life, then our lack of faith is a scandal to the world.

While it is infallibly true that God our Father desires all humankind to pursue the goal of the Gospel of peace, we all are indeed fallible in the choice of steps we take in trying to solve and to prevent conflicts on the road to final peace. But, we must have this conviction about peace. Only then can we make progress in our quest for more justice and a more solidly grounded peace.

Prayer

God of peace, we bless you for not abandoning a rebellious and war-prone world in its alienation and self-destructiveness. We thank you for sending us your only-begotten Son as Reconciler and Peacemaker. He has shown us the ways of peace and sealed his Gospel of peace by his precious blood.

Send forth your Spirit, so that we and all the world will understand how horrible is the fate which threatens humankind at this point in time. Bestow on us the fruits of the Spirit: truth, love, peace, and justice. Let your Spirit guide us on the path of peace.

Holy Spirit, help us to discover our inner resources for peace, which are your gifts to us. Activate these forces within us so that we may be credible witnesses for the Gospel of peace and the power of nonviolent action. Teach us to patiently and skillfully convince all of humanity that conversion to peace is most urgent in view of the threatening power blocks and dangerous ideologies which still dare to glorify violence, hatred, and claims of superiority in weapons of cruelty and destruction.

Lord, gird us with the weapons of love and peace, with invincible faith in the final victory of truth and love. Grant us the courage to commit ourselves to the Gospel of peace, whatever may be the necessary sacrifices. Let the Gospel of peace be "the shoes on our feet" to give us firm footing. May the power of your Spirit strengthen our faith as we strive for universal peace.

OTHER HELPFUL BOOKS
FROM LIGUORI PUBLICATIONS

IN PURSUIT OF HOLINESS
by Bernard Häring, C.SS.R.

This book offers wisdom, spiritual direction, and a sense of prayer. It shows you how to discover holiness in yourself and in the people you meet. With this discovery, you will be strengthened to give thanks even in time of trouble and be enlightened to exult in the beauty of God's creation and master plan. **$2.95**

MARY AND YOUR EVERYDAY LIFE
by Bernard Häring, C.SS.R.

Thirty-one simple "plain talk" meditations to help bring Mary and her Son into your everyday life. **$2.95**

Jesus' Pattern for a Happy Life:
THE BEATITUDES
by Marilyn Norquist

A beautiful, joy-filled book which invites you to consider the Beatitudes as a pattern for peace — a plan that *can* be followed in today's world. In the Sermon on the Mount, Jesus gave us a pattern for daily life in his Kingdom, a way to face troubles and problems and still find peace, hope, and joy. **$2.95**